The Bead Book

Sewing and Weaving with Beads

Ida-Merete Erlandsen

Hetty Mooi

D0573353

VNR VAN NOSTRAND REINHOLD COMPANY
New York   Cincinnati   Toronto   London   Melbourne

Van Nostrand Reinhold Company Regional Offices:
New York Cincinnati Chicago Millbrae Dallas

Van Nostrand Reinhold Company International Offices:
London Toronto Melbourne

This book was originally published in Danish and Dutch under the titles Kralen Weven en Weven med Kralen and Sy og Vaev med Perler by Cantecleer bv, De Bilt and Host and Sons Forlag, Copenhagen.

Translated from the Danish by Christine Hauch and from the Dutch by Danielle Adkinson.

Library of Congress Catalog Card Number: 74-3582
ISBN: 0–442–30052–2 (cloth)
ISBN: 0–442–30053–0 (paper)

This book is set in Univers, and printed in Great Britain by Jolly and Barber Ltd., Rugby, Warwickshire.

Published by Van Nostrand Reinhold Company Inc.,
450 West 33rd Street, New York N.Y. 10001
and Van Nostrand Reinhold Company Ltd.,
Molly Millar's Lane, Wokingham, Berkshire.

16 15 14 13 12 11 10 9 8 7 6 5 4 3 2 1
Library of Congress Cataloging in Publication Data
Erlandsen, Ida-Merete.
The Bead Book
Combined translation of Sy og vaev med perler, by I. -M. Erlandsen, and Kralen weven & weven met kralen, by H. Mooi.
1. Beadwork. I. Mooi, Hetty, joint author.
II. Erlandsen, Ida-Merete. Sy og vaev med perler.
III. Mooi, Hetty. Kralen weven & weven met kralen.
IV. Title.
TT860. E7313. 745.5. 74-3582.
ISBN 0-442-30052-2
ISBN 0-442-30053-0 (pbk.)

Contents

Introduction 4

1. Talking about beads 5

2. Historical uses of beads 10

3. What to do with beads 11

4. Strings of beads 16

5. 'Stretchy' strings of beads 18

6. Overlaid stitching 19

7. Beads in flat surfaces 21

8. The Greenland method 24

9. Beads on canvas 26

10. Embroidery and appliqué with beads 30

11. Knitting and crocheting with beads 36

12. Bead-weaving 38

13. Which beads to use 47

14. Plain weaving with beads 55

15. Bead-weaving in combination with other techniques 57

16. Finishing-off in bead-weaving 61

17. Bead-weaving on another loom 67

18. Practical pattern ideas 73

19. Weaving on round and square frames 88

20. More advanced bead-work 92

Introduction

Beads have been known to man for a long time and have played an important part in many cultures — as currency, for instance. Bead-work can be found all over the world; many civilizations have developed ingenious sewing and weaving techniques to produce beautiful articles.

This book is not intended as a history of the various kinds of bead-work; this subject has been treated extensively elsewhere. It is essentially a manual of techniques for use at home, at school, or in other craft groups. It explains many techniques of sewing and weaving with beads and provides practical suggestions, patterns and diagrams for making simple articles. Finally, however, it is up to the individual to experiment and to use his or her own judgement. This book will show you some of the possibilities.

Any well-stocked craft shop will sell beads, thread, fine wire, etc. Many department stores and needlework shops also stock materials for bead-work.

*A helmet from the Congo sewn with beads.
It is blackish-brown and white with red
edging.*

1. Talking about beads

Man-made ornaments have existed for a very long time. Very often these ornaments have either been composed entirely of beads or have contained them. Beads themselves have been made from many different kinds of materials in a great variety of shapes, sizes, and colours. It is difficult to establish the chronological order of the origin of different types of beads, since they have developed in different ways in different cultures, depending primarily on which materials were available in a given place. The following list will give you some indication of the different forms in which beads have developed.

Natural materials as beads

The first beads were probably made from natural objects which were perforated so that they could be threaded together to form a necklace. Some materials lend themselves immediately, without adaptation, to use as beads, while others have to be modified.

The most primitive bead-makers (and some present-day ones) used such materials as wood, bamboo, reeds, kernels, bones, seeds, shells, buds, vertebrae, teeth, leather, and stones. More modern cultures have made beads from metal and precious and semi-precious stones, but these were used only after the ability to work these harder materials was acquired. When this occurred varies from culture to culture, and is difficult to place exactly.

Ceramic beads

There are several kinds of ceramic beads: unbaked, baked, glazed, and porcelain. Unbaked beads date from the time of man's discovery of clay. At first clay was never baked, and the pots, ornaments, and beads made from it were simply left to dry in the sun.

Baked beads, which are waterproof, were invented later, and can be divided into the following categories:

(a) smooth beads

These were made by rolling a ball of clay in the palm of the hand. They are round or oval, and the hole is made before the clay is baked.

(b) shaped beads

These developed in two distinct ways. The first method is as follows: the clay is formed into a particular shape — a pipe or a ball, for example. A second layer of clay is added to the basic shape, which will turn a different colour from the first when fired. Parts of the top layer of clay are then removed to form a pattern. After baking, the difference in colour between the two layers becomes visible; where the sections of the outer layer have been removed, the inner layer shows through. This technique is called sgraffiato (fig. 1–2).

The second traditional way of making shaped beads is very similar to the first. Again the basic shape of the bead is made in a first clay, which is then covered with a layer of another clay which will bake a different colour from the first. This second clay, however, is not kneaded as a thick layer on to the first, as in the first process, but is applied as a thin paste made up of the clay mixed liberally with water. When dry, design motifs are scraped in the outer layer with a sharp tool, making parts of the inner layer visible again. The beads are then fired to show a contrast in colour. This method is called sgraffito (fig. 1–3). The difference between the two methods is that in the first whole sections are actually cut from the outer layer, whereas in the second the decorative motifs are less deeply cut. Beads made by both methods date from very early times, but they are quite rare now, and are found only in the excavations of old burial places and settlements. These beads are easy to make, however, and are a lot of fun to use in various ways.

The next step in the development of

ceramic beads was to glaze the beads. The discovery of how to control the glazing process was probably quite accidental. It might have happened during the baking of some clay article, when the presence of minerals at the location of the hot oven caused a glossy surface to form on the baking clay. But whatever the origin of glazing, craftsmen started to experiment with it and discovered, for instance, that a pot became waterproof if glazed on the inside and outside. Beautiful colours could be obtained by adding particular oxides during the glazing process. This technique was then applied to ceramic bead-making, often resulting in brilliant decorations. Sometimes finely-ground precious stones were mixed with the glazes to re-create the splendour of the whole stone.

Porcelain beads appeared much later; they were not made in Europe until around 1500 A.D., although they had been known and manufactured in China centuries earlier. They are made from a material which resembles clay but has a much finer composition. The beads made from this material are baked at very high temperatures, giving a much finer and more transparent appearance than the comparatively rough earthenware beads. Porcelain beads were often glazed and sometimes painted with brilliant colours.

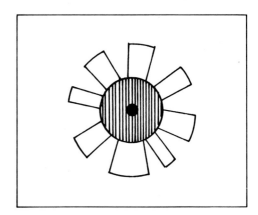

Fig. 1–2. Sgraffiato.

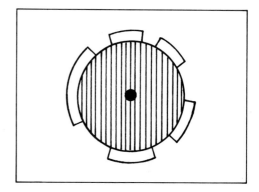

Fig. 1–3. Sgraffito.

Fig. 1–1. Machomboy mask from the Bakuba tribe, Congo (Country Life and Folklore Museum, Rotterdam). The mask is made from leather and woven fabric; the beads were threaded, then applied to the background. Several kinds of beads, including shells, were used for decoration, though the latter were sewn on individually.

Glass beads

This is the most important category of beads as far as this book is concerned, because glass beads (known as rocaille beads) are machine-made in all sizes and colours. They were a much-prized possession, even a form of exchange, in ancient times, and are now found all over the world in archaeological excavations. They were first manufactured in the 15th century B.C. in Egypt and the Near East.

Glass beads were first made by forming a globule of heated glass round an earthenware pipe. After the glass had cooled, the resultant bead was removed from the pipe, leaving a large centre hole which may still have had some clay in it (fig. 1–4). It was only after man had

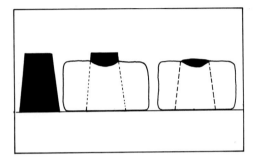

Fig. 1–4. Bead made from a molten drop of glass.

discovered how to shape glass that beads began to be spun. A heated ball of glass was pulled into a longer shape. This hardening but still slightly molten glass was wound on to a revolving metal bar. The glass was then pulled away from the metal, often leaving marks caused by the revolutions of the bar. Later the metal bar was allowed to revolve longer, which caused the marks to disappear and the beads to become round. These are called hand-wound beads (fig. 1–5). They were often beautifully coloured by adding various substances to the glass, such as metal oxides, (like copper), dye-producing minerals (like cobalt), or precious metals, (like gold).

Hand-cut beads were made quite differently. A number of small earthenware pipes were arranged on a kind of board. A bar of resilient though still slightly molten glass would then be wound round the pipe and cut. These beads are easy to recognize because they always

have a sharp protrusion where the glass has been cut, which has not melted into the rounded shape of the bead (fig. 1–6). They are also recognizable by the clay which frequently remains in the centre hole.

This method of making beads is a static and cumbersome process, and these beads are rather costly. In order to produce large quantities, beads were eventually machine-wound or moulded. But these later beads have less character than the hand-wound or hand-cut examples. A bead can be given an individual shape by pinching the glass while it is still molten.

There are various other types of beads which are perforated only after the beads themselves have been made. These beads can be recognized by the slight crookedness of their centre holes, which is due to the fact that they have been perforated from both directions. These blown glass beads have very thin walls and are very fragile. They are also very expensive because each one is hand-made.

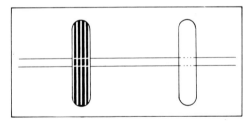

Fig. 1–5. Hand-wound bead.

Paper beads
These are made by winding a piece of paper round a knitting needle or a small pipe and then gluing both ends. When the glue is dry, the beads can be slipped off and are ready for use. It is advisable to use a quick-drying glue.

Beads can also be made from papier-mâché. Obviously such beads do not have to be spun, but are simply kneaded

round a small stick; they can even be
kneaded into shape first and perforated
afterwards.

Leather beads
These beads are very ancient and, like
paper beads, they must be wound round
some object.

Fig. 1—6. Hand-cut bead.

Synthetic beads
This type of bead did not come into
existence until synthetic materials such as
plastic were invented. Plastic beads are
characterized by an oily shine, and they
can be scratched by sharp objects.
Polystyrene beads are especially light
since they are made from what is in effect
a kind of foam. They can be shaped by
simple finger pressure, or even by picking
pieces out of them. They melt immediately
on exposure to a naked flame, as do
plastic beads.

Page 10.
*Fig. 2—1. Broad woven bead belt from
Nyasaland, South Africa (Country Life and
Folklore Museum, Rotterdam). The beads
which stand out slightly were sewn on
individually round the dark areas of the
pattern.*

2. Historical uses of beads

Beads have been and still are very often used as ornaments, principally to decorate the human form. Later this decoration acquired another dimension, i.e. to indicate social status; a rich person could acquire a large quantity of beads and therefore could decorate himself more elaborately. Beads were also used as a means of exchange and payment. They have very similar characteristics to coins; they are small, easy to carry, and last for a long time. Beads were widely used as currency at the height of the slave and gold trades. Glass beads first became prominent during the 15th century B.C. in Egypt and the Near East. By the time of the Romans, Alexandria had become one of the most important centres for the supply of beads. The art of glass-making was introduced to Italy from Byzantium, and by the 1st century A.D. the first bead factories in Europe were established in Venice and Murano. From there the technique eventually spread to the rest of Europe; two bead factories were finally opened in Amsterdam at the beginning of the 17th century, and Dutch merchants began to trade in these beads with America, Africa, and the Orient. In the 18th and 19th centuries, Bohemia and the Fichtel mountain region became important centres of bead production. Today Italy, West Germany, Yugoslavia, Israel, and India are the most important bead producers.

Apart from their use as decoration and as a means of exchange, beads were also used as an aid in calculation; the Chinese abacus, or counting frame, utilized hard wooden beads. In rosaries and other prayer-chains, beads assist in counting prayers. Beads are now used educationally in some schools (like Montessori) to teach arithmetic, either in the form of counting frames or as loose units. They are especially suited to teaching children arithmetic and even simple language functions. (See Chapter 13.)

3. What to do with beads

Techniques of bead-work

Beads can be used in a variety of ways: they can be threaded, braided, entwined, woven, knotted, worked with metal, knitted, crocheted, made into wreaths, or appliquéd.

The simplest way to work with beads is to thread them on a piece of string. By this method you can make a necklace, bracelet, ankle-band, bead-curtain, or lamp decoration. If several threads are plaited together the result closely resembles braiding. The beads can be threaded in open or closed order (figs. 3–1 and 2), and in sets of two, three, or more threads. In this way you can make purses, bags, curtains, necklaces, or decorations for articles of clothing.

Several threads can be used in knotting beads. All sorts of decorative effects can be achieved when beads are knotted together in open or closed weaves. Open knotting has a very loose appearance so that the background plays a part in the total effect (fig. 3–3). In closed knotting

the knot itself is very important, as well as the colour of the thread you use (fig. 3–3). For instance, you can start with a row of knotted braid, then a row of beads, and finally another row of braid. In this closed kind of work the beads and the structure of the knotting form a unity.

Bead-work that utilizes knotting is much stronger than threaded work, since every knot secures a whole group of beads. If one thread breaks the whole fabric does not fall to pieces, as is usually the case with bead-work which is merely threaded.

If you want to work in beads and metal, you can thread the beads on a strip of wire instead of string. You can buy these strips ready-made or make them up yourself. There are two sorts of metal wire which are useful for this purpose: one has a tiny knob at the end so that the bead cannot slide off (fig. 3–4); the other has a little eye-hole at the end. You can slip a bead along one of these wires and then bend the end round into

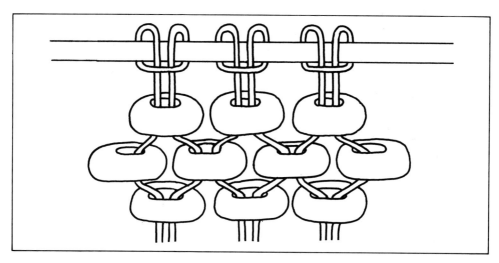

Fig. 3–1. Closed threading.

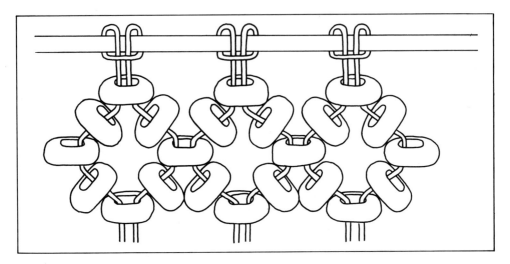

Fig. 3–2. Open threading.

an eye-shape so that the bead is made secure (fig. 3–5). By linking the eyes of a number of such strips of wire, which are much easier to make than the first type, it is possible to make both simple and more complex articles.

When beads are used in knitting or crocheting you must decide first of all whether the article has to be washable. If so, it is best to use metal or glass beads; otherwise, any kind of bead can be used. In knitting the bead is always placed on the loop connecting two purled stitches (fig. 3–6). In crocheting the bead usually lies on the reverse side of the work, though it is possible to place it on the upper side; this, however, is quite difficult to do. When knitting or crocheting, the beads must be threaded before you can start work. If you want a bead in a particular position, slip it forward, secure it with a stitch, and then continue. This makes it possible to make all sorts of patterns when knitting or crocheting.

When sewing beads it is advisable to sew them separately. Individual beads can be emphasized by embroidery, or they can be sewn in groups, thus creating entire decorative motifs composed of beads. If you first thread the beads and then sew the threaded length on to some background material, you are really carrying out appliqué work in beads. The only disadvantage of this method is that all the beads will fall off if the thread breaks. But if they are sewn on separately, the damage is limited to a single bead.

In the following chapters, many of these techniques of beadwork will be discussed in detail, with diagrams and illustrations to assist you in following the patterns yourself.

Setting-up

Before you begin to work, you should arrange the beads in an orderly fashion. The most organized way to sort your beads is to group them according to size and colour. You can buy transparent boxes or use empty plastic containers to keep your beads in. Then you can spread the colours out in front of you like a palette while you work.

It is also advisable to draw a diagram of the pattern before you begin. You can draw it on graph paper or any other squared paper. There is only one thing that you should remember: beads are not

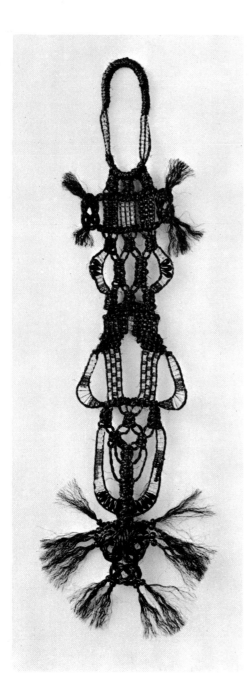

circular when you look at them from the side, and a pattern is often slanted in this fashion when sewn with thread. Thus something like a cross-stitch pattern will work out more elongated than it appears in the diagram. The patterns illustrated in this book should give you an idea of the many kinds of designs that you can create. The more work you have done and the more techniques you have mastered, the easier it will be to work imaginatively with beads.

Beads, needles and thread

Beads are so easy to handle and so tempting to work with that children can learn how to use them too. Small children find it easiest to work with wooden beads which have large holes and are simple to thread with a darning needle. Elastic thread, which is available in several colours, is suitable for wooden beads, both for threading them and for sewing them together.

When working with glass beads the most difficult job can be threading the needle, since you have to use a very thin needle to get it through the holes in the smallest rocaille beads. (In this case a special needle threader can solve the problem.) Needles nos. 9–12 are suitable. Thread them with double sewing silk, nylon thread, or thin crochet yarn D.M.C. no. 100, all of which can be used for both sewing and weaving. When weaving the very tiniest glass beads, the warp or long thread should be D.M.C. no. 100 and the weft or weaving thread double sewing silk or nylon thread. Only needle no. 12 will go through the holes in these

Fig. 3–3. Macramé wall decoration. Beads were woven in between the slightly separated threads, creating a greater variety of colourful areas. This work contains both open and closed knotting, which emphasizes both the beads and the knots.

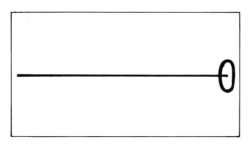

Fig. 3–4. Nail-wire.

beads. From time to time you should rub wax into the thread you are using for sewing or weaving, so that it doesn't wear thin. Strong cotton thread or twine and a long darning needle are best for large glass beads. For bugle beads you should use double sewing silk or thin crochet yarn such as D.M.C. no. 100.

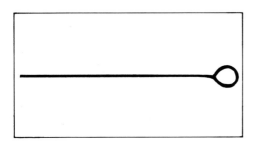

Fig. 3–5. Eye-wire.

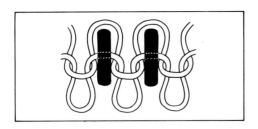

Fig. 3–6. A bead on the linking loop of two purled stitches.

Opposite.
Fig. 3–7. A small selection of the many shapes of beads available commercially.

Fig. 3–8. This shows the great variation in size of the most common glass (rocaille) beads. Those third from the left, known as Greenland beads, are probably the most popular.

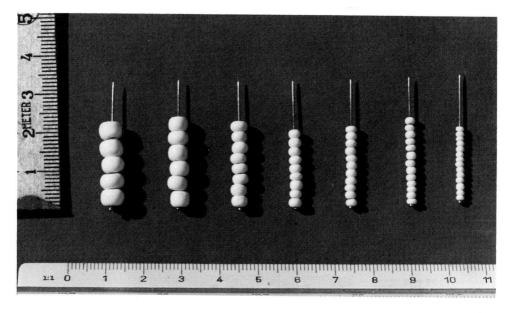

4. Strings of beads

The simplest way to put beads together is to thread them on a string. It is especially important to choose a suitable string for the different kinds and qualities of beads.

If you are using particularly heavy or sharp-edged beads it will be worth your while to use nylon thread or fishing line. To protect your beads further you can make a knot in the thread between each bead. This has two advantages: it brings out and separates the individual beads from each other, and it prevents all the beads from falling off at once if the thread breaks. (This is a good place to mention that if you are cutting an old necklace to make a new one, for example, you should do it over a tray or a large dish so that all the beads do not spill.)

In fig. 4—2 you can see a simple bead necklace of two rows. Large glass beads $\frac{1}{5}$ in. (5 mm.) in size have been threaded with twine. In the gaps there are knots in the twine. To make a rhythmic pattern four beads were alternated in one colour first with two free-standing white beads with knots between them, and then with four beads in another colour, and so on. It doesn't take much to make a bead necklace distinctive so long as you have some feeling for the importance of variation.

The photograph also shows a hot-plate, which once again has been made from $\frac{1}{5}$ in. (5 mm.) beads sewn together. It was sewn by hand as described in fig. 7—1, diagrams 7—9, using very coarse cotton thread. The bead border was sewn on afterwards in loops.

Fig. 4—1. Many southern countries have a custom of decking donkeys and mules with collars of very coarse coloured beads, always with an emphasis on blue, which is supposed to protect the animals against the 'evil eye'.

Opposite.
Fig. 4—2. 1. A hot-plate of large white, green, light blue, and orange glass beads. 2. A coarse string of beads threaded on twine. The groups of different colours are separated by two white beads and three knots.

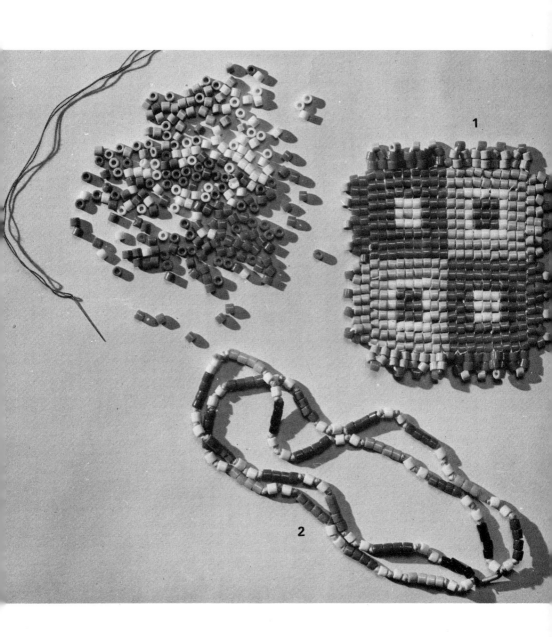

5. 'Stretchy' strings of beads

Fig. 5–1, diagrams 1, 2, and 3, sets out an easy technique for sewing a bead chain. Wooden beads and elastic thread are ideal for this kind of sewing.

Diagram 1 shows how to start by drawing three beads on to the thread, then crossing both ends of the thread through the fourth bead. Add one bead on each thread, followed by another cross bead, and so on.

In diagrams 2 and 3, the number of beads between the cross beads is increased. A further variation is to make the cross bead a different colour or size than the beads at the sides.

Diagram 4 shows another way of putting beads together. String a number of beads on to a single thread, then draw the thread through the first bead again to make a little circle. Next put on the centre bead, which can be a different size or colour than the surrounding beads. Fasten the thread into the circle again through one of the beads, forming a new circle.

Note that the thread passes through the connecting bead three times, so you must use beads which have large holes, and a rather thin thread.

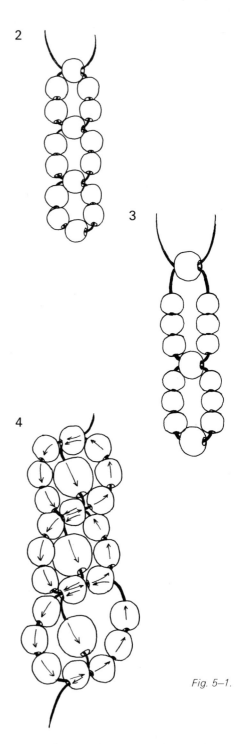

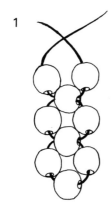

Fig. 5–1.

6. Overlaid stitching

Overlaid stitching, which is also called Sumatra stitching, is a technique of sewing on strings of beads. It has been practised in many parts of the world and has been applied particularly to stylized geometric and flower motifs.

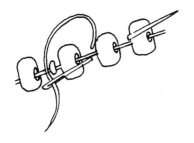

Fig. 6–1.

For overlaid stitching you need two needles and two double threads of sewing silk. Thread one of these with beads; use the other to sew the rows of beads across the first thread with small stitches (fig. 6–1). It is a free and fascinating technique, both for contoured sewing and for filling out panels, and it will look just as lovely on fabric, raffia, or leather.

The strong geometric patterns in the betel bags from Sumatra (fig. 6–2) are a good example of the timeless quality of designs with attractive colours and dimensions. The two bags could just as easily have been made today as many years ago.

You can use small or large round glass beads or bugle beads for overlaid stitching. Gold and silver beads may also be used, but they tend to tarnish. Articles trimmed with these beads should be kept in dark tissue paper. Glass beads are available in a wide range of colours, and they will withstand the stress of daily life much better.

Overlaid stitching can also be used to make buttons. There are several ways to do this. For example, you can make a round button out of leather drawn round a plastic curtain ring, and then sew the beads in a pattern inside the ring. The button will wear well because the edge of the ring protects the bead motif. Machine-made fabric buttons can also be decorated with bead-work, but they are not quite so durable. Tiny bead motifs glued on to a double layer of leather with a loop sewn on the back also make fine buttons.

Larger articles like place-mats can be personalized by trimming them with patterns of overlaid stitching.

Fig. 6–2. Betel bags from Nias on the west coast of Sumatra.

Fig. 6–3. A selection of decorative buttons;
the round ones are sewn with overlaid
stitching, while the rectangular ones are
woven. Small pieces of work are ideal for
practice and experimentation.

7. Beads in flat surfaces

There are two basic methods of sewing beads together so that they will lie in flat surfaces. In the first technique the beads are placed alternately like bricks; in the second the beads lie next to each other almost as if they were woven.

The alternating method

The first method is explained in fig. 7–1, diagrams 1–3.

Diagram 1 shows how to fasten the end bead and draw another eight beads on to the string. This means that the

Fig. 7–1.

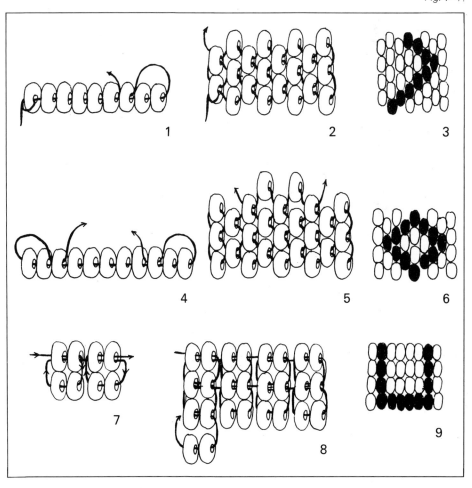

Fig. 7–2.

finished work will be eight beads wide, since the ninth bead is shifted up into the second row. Skip the eighth bead, and pass the thread through the seventh. Then add a new bead on to the thread and pass the thread through the fifth bead, add a new bead, through the third, and so on. Continue along this row, then turn and sew back. The procedure will be clear from the diagram.

Fig. 7–1, diagrams 4–6 shows a variation by which you can use the same technique with two threads. The threads will always cross over each other in the centre bead, after which the left-hand needle sews alternately out to the end, turns, and returns to the centre bead. Follow the same procedure with the right-hand needle. The advantage of this method is that there will always be an uneven number of beads in the width, which makes it easier to work in a pattern. If you are only using one thread and an even number of beads, the pattern may

Fig. 7–3.

end up running diagonally or completely vertically. If you compare diagrams 3 and 6 in fig. 7–1 you can see the difference quite clearly.

The consecutive method

The second basic method is to sew the beads together in pairs as shown in fig. 7–1, diagrams 7 and 8. This can be done either lengthways or across the strip of beads. The first row you sew may be slightly difficult to manage, but by the time you have reached the third or fourth row there is something to hold on to, which makes it easier to sew the rest.

As you can see from the diagram, the thread goes through each bead several times, which means that the work will be firm and secure, but of course this kind of sewing is unsuitable for beads with small holes.

Figs. 7–2 and 3 show pendants of wooden beads made by the methods described below.

The pendant at the top was made by the technique shown in fig. 7–1, diagrams 1–3, and it has a diagonal motif in the centre section. Two strings, each twelve beads long, connect the centre to the oblong side sections from which the string continues round the neck. A bead fringe, sewn on to the centre part, is added afterwards.

The lower pendant was sewn according to the method shown in fig. 7–1, diagrams 7–9. Here the middle section is divided by a checked pattern consisting of four white and four black beads. At the bottom of this panel there is a fringe of small beads. The double chain is sewn together from large black and white beads in groups of four, as in the centre motif. In between there are short connecting rows of slightly smaller beads. The piece which goes round the neck is a single chain in the same pattern.

Bracelets and anklets can be made in the same way, but you should use elastic thread so that they will slip easily over hand or foot.

8. The Greenland method

There is no end to the number of ways that you can sew beads together. But whatever method you use, you should remember one important rule: the beads must be of the same size or the whole work will look messy. The beads should also have a good 'face'; they should have large, open holes so that you can sew three, four, or five times through them. Use a no. 10 needle and D.M.C. crochet yarn no. 100 or nylon thread, which you can buy in many colours. Nylon thread is strong but smooth so you will have to fasten it very securely. This is done partly by going back into the row of beads and partly by sewing a button-hole stitch between the beads occasionally.

The Greenland method is a development of the method shown in fig. 7–1, diagrams 1–3. Instead of sewing with one bead in the gap, draw four beads into the thread. In fig. 8–2, diagram 1, the two

 1

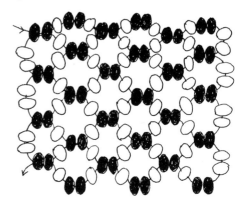

2

Fig. 8–1. Detail of a classic Greenland collar.

3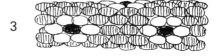

centre beads have been shaded to show which beads must be sewn into again to give a patterned effect.

Just as you can sew backwards and forwards, you can also sew round. Fig. 8–2, diagram 2 shows how you can start by sewing twelve beads into a circle, and then go on to add one bead at a time close to the circle. Fig. 8–2, diagram 3 shows a little flower motif made with this technique. You can continue this little rope of beads round and round to make a bracelet, a choker, or a belt.

In fig. 8–3 you can see two round pendants which were mounted on interfacing material. To make the circular shapes, start by sewing one bead in the

Fig. 8–2.

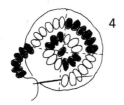

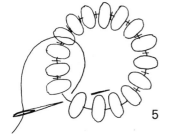

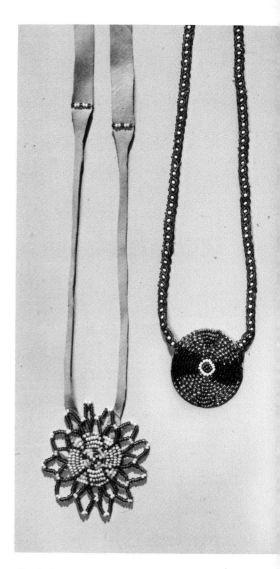

centre, and then work one ring of beads after another outward from there. Draw the beads on to the thread, lay them round the centre bead, and stitch through the first two beads again, as in fig. 8–2, diagram 4. Then sew the circle firmly to the backing with small stitches between the beads so that the thread is fastened to the backing, as in fig. 8–2, diagram 5.

Before you start you can draw a circle on the interfacing, and sketch in a pattern with a crayon.

Trim the interfacing when you have finished the bead-work, and glue it to a piece of thin cardboard. Sew a thin piece of glove leather on the back round the edge.

The chain is made by following the method shown in fig. 5–1, diagram 1. The only difference in this case is that all the beads are the same size and the whole chain is lined with leather. The pendant

Fig. 8–3. Two mounted pendants. The pendant on the left has a jagged edge in the Greenland style.

on the left is hung on a narrow strip of leather. The circular centre section has a spiky edge with open points, as in fig. 8–2, diagram 6.

9. Beads on canvas

For anyone who likes cross-stitching on canvas or other kinds of material where the threads are easy to count, bead-sewing may prove an interesting variation. The beads will lie diagonally since the stitch is similar to half a cross-stitch or petit point, so you can start with patterns which will not be changed by the shape of the beads, as often happens with other techniques (fig. 9–1, diagram 1). Use fine or coarse material depending on the size of the beads, and sew over two threads with a no. 10 needle and double sewing silk. Rub the silk with wax so that the thread does not slip.

Stitch carefully and firmly, passing through each bead several times. A bead hanging loose on its thread in the middle of a finished piece of work looks sloppy. Make sure that you fasten the thread securely at the beginning and the end. Sew the edge firmly, twice through each bead.

To make the work smooth after you have finished sewing dampen it with water, and then stretch it out tightly on a wooden board with drawing pins. When it is dry you can glue it on to some other article as decoration (a spectacles case or a little box for jewels, playing-cards, cigarettes, etc.), as in fig. 9–2. If you are using the bead-work for a box lid you should add a supporting framework of strong cardboard or very thin wood, which you also glue on. You may wish to make a bell-pull from beads, in which case the weight of the beads alone is sufficient to support the work.

It takes longer to sew with beads than with yarn, but the work will always look fresh and new because the beads do not fade.

The long bugle beads which were so often used to decorate dresses in the twenties are ideally suited for making mosaics on canvas (fig. 9–1, diagram 2). In fig. 9–2, photograph 4 you can see a pendant with long bugle beads of various

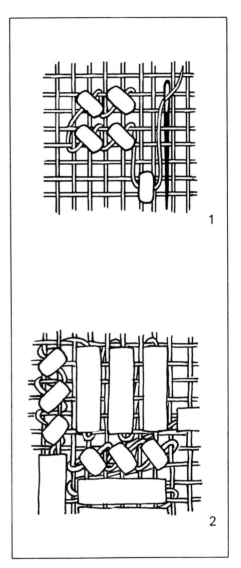

Fig. 9–1.

Fig. 9–2. Sewing beads on canvas offers opportunities for decorating many useful objects. 1. Box for playing cards. 2. Small purse. 3. Spectacles case. 4. Bugle bead pendant. 5. Cigarette box.

lengths, thicknesses, and colours sewn on to canvas. Where the beads are not so long, small round beads in contrasting colours have been added, which makes an interesting change in the pattern. The piece of canvas is mounted on black leather, and the chain is sewn with beads drawn on to thick cotton thread.

The background to the playing card king (fig. 9–2, photograph 1) is made of white beads and scattered, single turquoise beads. The king's cape and mouth are scarlet, as are the heart and diamond. The king's hair, beard, profile, and legs, and the spade and club, are black. The face and hands are pink, the tunic is green, and the crown and sceptre are gold. The upper section of the king's robe is sewn with green and white beads, the centre with yellow, and the lower section with black and white beads.

The little purse (fig. 9–2, photograph 2)

Fig. 9–3. Pattern diagram for the playing card king which decorates the card box in Fig. 9–2, photograph 1.

28

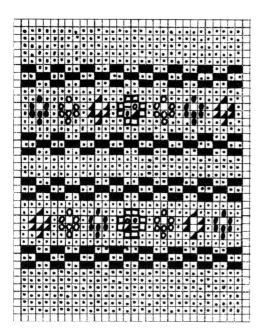

Fig. 9–4. Diagram for the purse in Fig. 9–2, photograph 2.

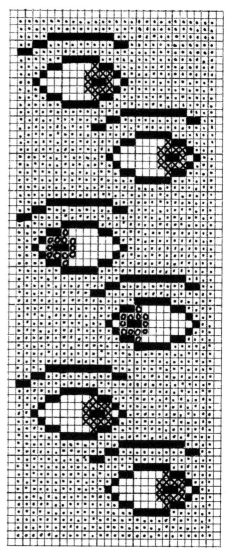

Fig. 9–5. Diagram for the spectacles case in Fig. 9–2, photograph 3.

has a strong turquoise background colour and brighter, clearer colours in the small motifs.

The background to the spectacles case (fig. 9–2, photograph 3) is bright yellow, and the eyes are black and white with alternating brown, blue, and green pupils.

10. Embroidery and appliqué with beads

Embroidery

Beads can be sewn on to fabric either singly or in groups. If you are sewing on only one bead, it must be large enough to stand out as a point of focus. The way in which it is sewn on is also very important, since the stitches reinforce the final effect of the bead. The most suitable stitch for this operation is the tacking stitch. Choose a bead with a large hole — a ring bead, for instance — and secure it firmly to the background material with several stitches. (Six stitches will produce a very beautiful effect.)

Groups or rows of beads must also be sewn individually on to the background material but placed very close to one another. Afterwards, thread cotton through the beads so that they lie in the same direction. Groups of beads can be formed into all sorts of interesting patterns, whereas single beads tend to give a speckled appearance to the work.

Appliqué

To do appliqué work, first string a number of beads along a thread. This row of beads can then be sewn as a unit on to the background material. The thread which runs through the beads should be secured in a number of places with small stitches, using a different colour of thread. This method has one disadvantage in comparison to individual sewing; if the thread breaks, all the beads fall off instead of just a single bead.

Both methods are frequently used to decorate clothes, and in the past appliqué with beads has also been used to decorate ceremonial masks, head-dresses, and other symbolic objects (fig. 10–1).

Old beaded articles have a magical, fairy-tale quality; they can be given new life if they are reworked in untraditional ways.

The evening bag in fig. 10–2 is made of hand-woven material and trimmed with fringes of beads. The design and the beads themselves come from a 1920's dress, when closely-set rows of beads were in fashion.

Bead fringes are also a familiar decoration on old lampshades. They were usually made of clear, coloured glass beads. Light through glass beads can produce beautiful effects; the beads become an illuminated border, for example, if you sew a selection of differently coloured and sized beads to the bottom of a window shade in rows. (These can be sewn by the Greenland method explained in Chapter 8.)

Embroidery and appliqué with thread and beads appeal to the imagination in many ways. You can experiment further by sewing small beads over the holes of everyday objects like mother-of-pearl buttons or snap fasteners. The possibilities are endless; there is only one rule to bear in mind, whatever kind of beadwork you are doing: it should have the effect of making you want to 'look at it with your hands'.

Fig. 10–1. King's head-dress from Dahomey, West Africa (Country Life and Folklore Museum, Rotterdam). Faces, probably of symbolic significance, were added to the front and back of the head-dress. The bead-work consists of strings of beads which have been sewn on to the background material to form geometrical patterns.

Borders

The repeated motif or border is a perennial device which is open to infinite variation. One development was the stylization of naturalistic objects (often the original source of inspiration), eventually transforming them into something purely decorative and often unrecognizable, and thereby giving them an entirely new life. Borders of this kind are found all over the world. Often they consist of single sequins sewn on with little beads. Such tiny, glistening accents have a very delicate effect, much like that of the small mirrors sewn into Indian fabrics and clothes.

Bead-work of this type is most beautiful when the patterns and colour combinations are simple; a mixture of chance ideas hastily put together is hardly attractive. The rhythm created by an ordered and regular repetition can approach a 'restrained splendour' which is certainly the highest aspiration for any border!

If you are working with wooden beads in conjunction with embroidery stitches, you can use the same thread for both. For glass beads, however, you need a thread that is very strong but also thin enough to pass through the holes in the beads. Since this kind of thread is not suitable for embroidery, you will have to use separate yarns.

Mosaic

The brilliant colours of glass beads suggest yet another technique, glass mosaic. The mosaic can be glued on to a firm surface to make it more durable, although it should not be exposed to constant handling. Use the following method: dab a little glue on to the surface, and set the beads in place with tweezers or a pin stuck into the hole of the bead. The same method can be used to make small, primitive motifs on place-cards and match-boxes, as well as slightly more permanent things like a calendar picture, for example.

Colour Plate 1. Belts made with different sizes of beads. Bits of plain weaving in matching colours were scattered throughout. The red belt has both rectangular and triangular openings (formed by inserting ringlets) and cylinder-shaped beads which open out the threads.

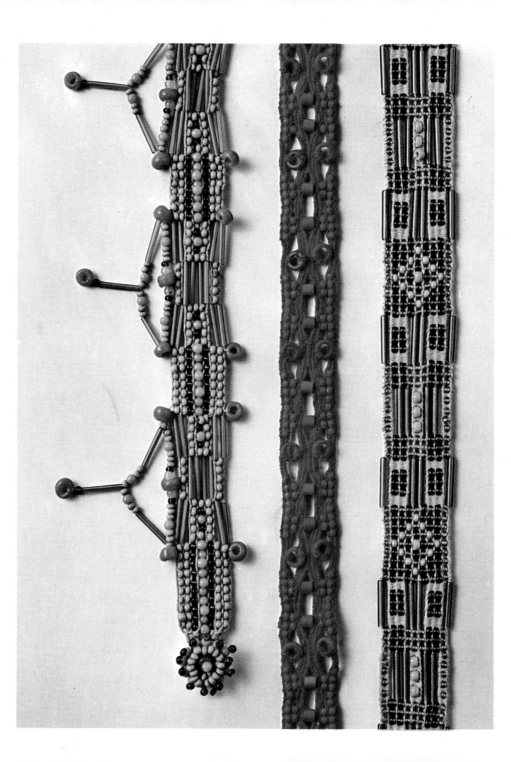

Fig. 10–2. Handbag decorated with bead fringes from the 1920's.

Fig. 10–3. Birds made from sequins.

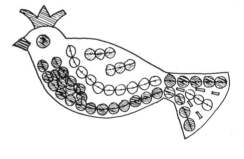

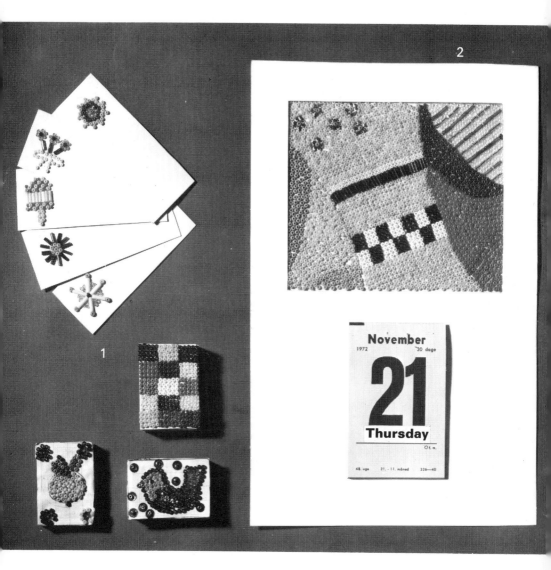

Fig. 10–4. 1. Small bead decorations applied to place-cards and match-boxes with hobby glue. 2. A calendar with an abstract bead motif.

11. Knitting and crocheting with beads

Knitting traditionally has been one of the most popular techniques of working with beads. Many examples of this kind of bead-work have been preserved, since it is practically indestructible. The traditional bead purse shown in fig. 11–1 has the words 'nie leer' ('never empty') knitted as a finishing touch above the familiar rose pattern.

Knitting

The simplest and possibly the most attractive method of knitting with beads is to draw on to knitting yarn a number of beads, all of the same colour but different from that of the yarn. Gather the beads together on to the yarn before you start the actual knitting. Whenever you need a bead for the pattern, slip it along the yarn, and knit it in on the right side of the work. You will soon learn how far along the yarn to slide the bead so that it is in the right place for your own knitting rhythm (fig. 11–2).

If you want to use several different colours of beads in a design, follow the pattern back to front.

To add a border of beads to a sweater, a bag, or anything at all, knit a narrow strip of beads separately and sew it on afterwards. In this way you can get a raised effect at the same time.

Crochet

To crochet with beads you can use cotton, silk, or twine. Just as in knitting, draw the beads on to the yarn before you start crocheting.

Work in double crochet, putting the hook through the back of the preceding loop. If you are working in a circle for a bag or a hat, simply continue round and round. If, on the other hand, you are making a flat, even piece of work, you will have to break off the yarn at the end of every row so that the stitches always lie in the same direction. The easiest way to crochet in the beads is on the reverse side, but this does make what would normally be the reverse side the upper side (fig. 11–3). You can crochet in a bead with each stitch or jump stitches to make a pattern, as in knitting with beads.

The twine bag in fig. 11–3 is decorated with two colours of wooden beads which are crocheted in irregular rows.

Fig. 11–1. This bead purse is knitted with the optimistic text 'nie leer' ('never empty'). The purse comes from Germany and dates from the 19th century.

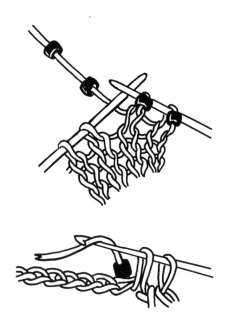

Fig. 11–2.

Fig. 11–3. A bag crocheted in twine with inserted rows of wooden beads. The beads are in two shades of violet, which go well with the natural twine.

12. Bead-weaving

Looms specifically designed for bead-weaving are now available commercially, but they can be expensive for schools or craft groups. However, it is very easy to make your own loom. Weaving probably began with the simple technique of hanging fibrous materials from a branch or some other naturally curved object and stretching them by fastening heavy stones at the bottom as weights, and primitive looms continue to offer possibilities for creative weaving. This book will show you how to make two kinds of looms, and techniques that can be used with each of them. (Both are equally suitable for right- and left-handed people, since it does not matter which side you weave from.) The first loom is discussed in Chapters 12—16 and the second in Chapters 17—18.

Fig. 12—1. Woven bead loin-cloth with a geometrical pattern from Guyana, South America (Country Life and Folklore Museum, Rotterdam). The warp threads end in strings of beads decorated with nuts.

For the first loom you will need a strip of Formica, which is obtainable from a craft supplies shop. This material can be cut easily to any size with a small saw, and it can often be bought in remnants, which makes it quite cheap. Formica is especially suitable for groups since the strips take up very little storage space. Another advantage of Formica is that it is at the same time reasonably strong and very flexible. These characteristics are particularly useful in a bead-loom because the Formica must be bent slightly to set up the warp. Make sure that you bend the Formica carefully along the grooves on the back; otherwise it may break across. It is advisable to buy a good quality of Formica which is easy to bend back into shape. Formica is preferable to other materials such as hardboard or cardboard since it does not become flaccid once it has been bent. The tension remains constant, which means that you do not have to make indentations in the Formica or use nails to hold the threads a set distance apart. When you have completed the first part of the weave, you can bend the Formica slightly to slip back the finished part, and start weaving at the front again.

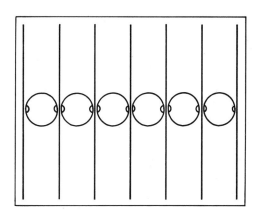

Fig. 12–3. Six beads fit between seven warp threads.

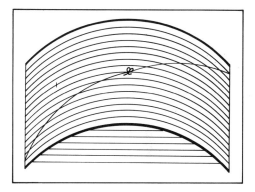

Fig. 12–4. The beginning and the end of the threads are knotted together.

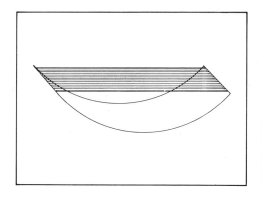

Fig. 12–2. Warp set up by the winding method.

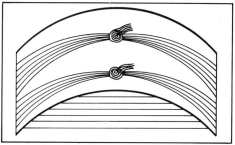

Fig. 12–5. Warp threads knotted behind the loom.

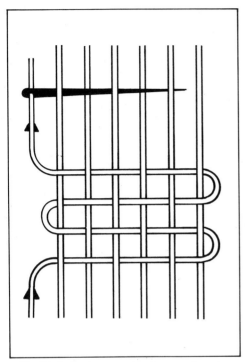

Fig. 12–6. Casting-on with six warp threads. (Above.)

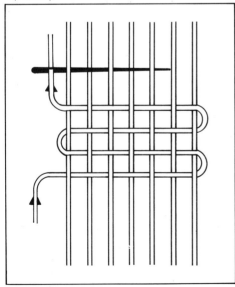

Any kind of thread can be used for the warp, as long as it is not stretchable. If a thread is stretchable it will snap when the weave is removed from the Formica.

You should test each thread for strength before using it. If you use a thin thread for the warp, double the thickness to make sure that it is strong enough. The thickness of the warp threads has nothing to do with the size of the beads (with large beads the distances between the threads simply become greater); it is governed only by what you want to make. If you want to make a belt, for example, you should use a thicker warp thread than you would use for a necklace. Use a fairly thick coloured thread if the warp is to form a part of the weave, and a completely colourless nylon thread if it is to remain in the background. The best thickness to work with is 0·20, which is available at craft and fishing equipment shops.

While the warp does not affect the thickness of the weft (which passes under and over the warp), the weft itself must be thin enough to go at least twice through the holes of the beads.

There are two ways of setting up the weft on your Formica loom: you can either wind the thread round the Formica or knot separate threads at the back. Both methods will be explained.

The winding method
First cover the short end of the piece of Formica with Sellotape to prevent the threads of the warp from breaking. To make the warp, bend the Formica slightly and wind a single long thread round it (fig. 12–2). The number of times it is wound round determines the number of warp threads; always allow one more warp thread than the number of beads in each row.

Fig. 12–7. Casting-on with seven warp threads.

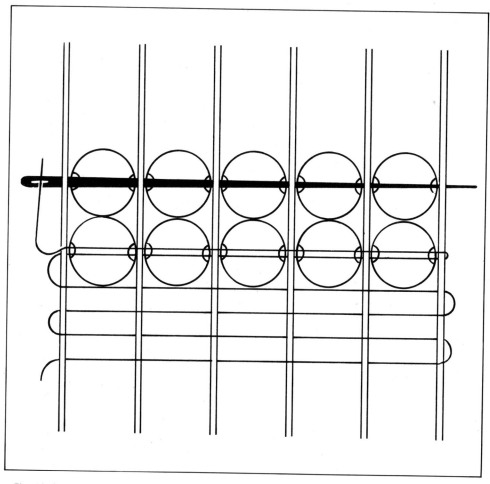

Fig. 12—8. Bead-weaving.

If your weave is six beads wide, for example, you must have seven warp threads (fig. 12—3), because each bead is always placed between two warp threads. While you are winding the thread hold on to the end at the back of the Formica. When you have wound the thread round the Formica a sufficient number of times, cut it, and knot the end of the thread to the beginning (fig. 12—4).

In this method the length of the warp is determined entirely by the size of the piece of Formica. The working length of thread is limited to the amount that can pass in front of and behind the Formica. You must make absolutely sure that the warp threads are long enough for your needs (including finishing-off).

42

Opposite.

Fig. 12–9. A plain woven bag decorated with bead-weaving. The combination is particularly noticeable on the handle, where plain and bead-weaving were alternated. The bag itself was woven on a wide piece of Formica, and the handle on another longer piece.

The knotting method

In the knotting method the length of thread may exceed the amount that can pass round the Formica. To use this method, first cut separate pieces of thread in the length you require, which is determined by the amount needed for the work itself plus finishing-off. The threads are not wound in one continuous length round the Formica, but instead are knotted together, no more than seven at a time, at the back of the Formica. If you need more warp threads, ten, for example, you can make two groups of five (fig. 12–5). The length of thread available for the warp can be at least doubled, because of the substantial reserve in the knots at the back of the Formica. The advantage of this method is that you can unfasten the work during the weaving to see whether the warp is long enough or to add an extra piece to the weave. It is important in macramé, which requires a lot of thread, to have a sufficient amount in reserve. You can even slip beads on the warp threads before you start weaving if you want the warp to form part of the actual weave. Be very careful about the relationship between the holes in the beads and the thickness of the warp thread; the holes must be large enough not only for the warp thread to pass through, but also for the needle and the weft thread to move from one motif to another (fig. 12–12).

When adding beads to the warp threads, determine in advance how many are needed in the motif, as well as the length that they will occupy. You can work in this instance with long bugle beads, varying them in other places with, say, four small beads (colour plate 1). As you work, slip each bead in place as needed. After you have added the beads to the warp threads, knot the threads behind the Formica. The beads and thread will look rather untidy, but once everything is in order behind the Formica and the beads have all been gathered on the concave work side, you can start weaving.

The weaving itself is a very simple operation. First space out the warp threads so that the beads will fit easily between them. Before actually beginning to weave with the beads, weave the weft several times through the warp to make sure that it is secure. This operation is particularly important, because you will need enough thread left over to cast-off the beginning when the weave is completed; this section of the weft, however, is very easily undone. When you choose the thread for the weft, you must obviously take into account the size of the hole in the bead, which must be large enough to allow the needle and thread to pass through it at least twice. The weaving is begun by passing the weft underneath the warp in such a way as to finish with the weft passing over the last warp thread on the last row. A certain amount of calculation is involved at this point, because the operation differs slightly depending on whether there is an even or an odd number of threads. For example, if you have six threads, then begin your fourth pass with the weft under the first warp thread, over the second, under the third, etc., until the weft passes over the sixth warp (fig. 12–6). But if you have seven warp threads, then begin the fourth pass over the first thread and finish over the seventh (fig. 12–7).

Now you are ready to begin weaving the beads. Remember that you always need one more warp thread than the number of beads you are weaving. It is a good idea to make a plan of your design on squared paper, on which you can also indicate the colour of the beads you are

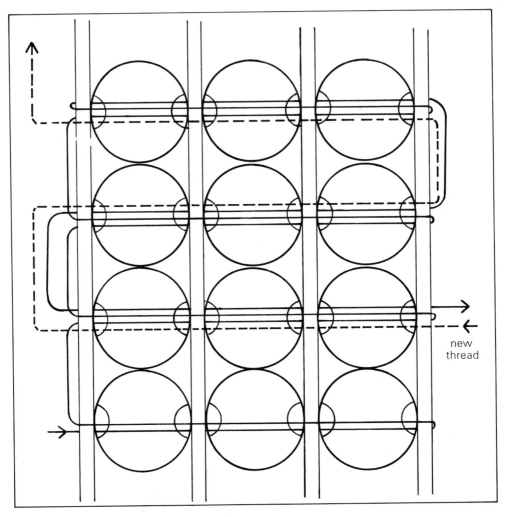

new
thread

*Fig. 12–10. Casting-on and -off with old and
new threads.*

using. Thread the weft through a long needle, and slip the first row of beads on to this needle. Pass the needle with the beads underneath the warp, pressing the beads upwards into the spaces between the warp threads. (It is helpful to put your finger underneath the warp to hold the beads in place while pulling the needle and thread through the holes.) Then thread the needle back through the beads, this time passing the weft over the warp (fig. 12–8). In this way the beads are arranged between the warp threads in a neat row. If you do not want the weft to show in the finished work, you should use nylon thread, which is also very strong.

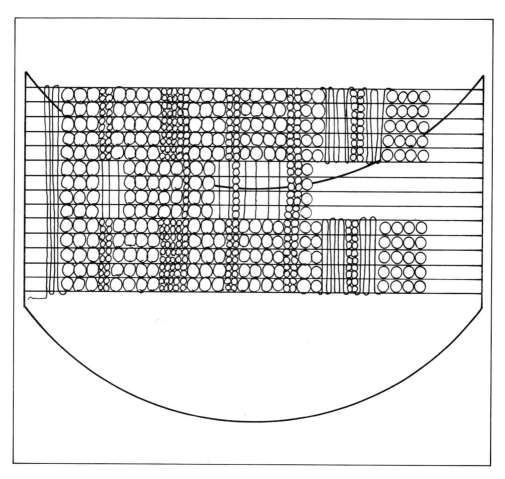

Fig. 12–11. Setting up the weave on a piece of Formica.

After completing the first row, simply continue weaving in exactly the same manner until the pattern is complete. The pattern should stand out from the background. Keep your work neat and restrained; mixing several designs in the same article can look very untidy, and too many colours can make a pattern too loud.

When the weft starts to run out, it must be cast-off and a new thread started. Make sure that you have about 4 in. (10 cm.) to thread back through some of

the beads already woven. If a short length of thread remains sticking out, cut it back flush to the nearest bead. The weft thread should be started where the old thread was cut off and passed back through the row until the casting-off point is reached.

Now you are ready to set up specific sorts of weaves on the warp. Arrange the Formica in front of you with the concave side and the warp uppermost. The knot holding the warp is in the centre of the convex side of the Formica.

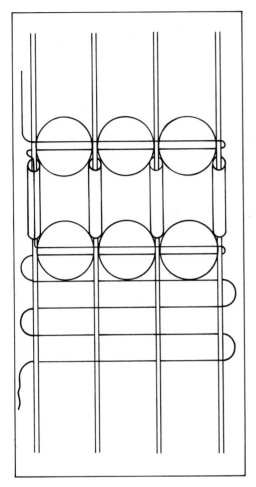

will form the collar part of the choker (fig. 12–11). These bands are woven separately until they reach the correct length and are ready to be cast-off.

If you have threaded some beads on the warp before starting the weaving, you can slip these beads forward to wherever they are needed. Sometimes, however, you may find that these beads lie in the path of the weft. If this happens, you must thread the weft up through the holes of the beads and then continue weaving as before (fig. 12–12). If you want to weave a choker without a medallion, weave one band first, taking care to leave enough thread to cast-off the weave. When doing this kind of work it is best to use the knotting method of securing the warp, since this ensures that a sufficient amount of thread will remain.

When the band is completed take it off the Formica to finish it off properly. This can be done either by sewing a decorative clasp on each end of the warp or with macramé (colour plate 2). In the latter method the thread ends are worked together to form an end-piece. Naturally, in both cases the closing and finishing-off of the choker are done on the outside so that it hangs properly.

A belt can be made by a similar technique, simply by widening and lengthening the weave. Here too it is best to knot the warp threads behind the Formica, especially if you want to do more tacking or macramé between the bead-weaving. This is discussed more fully in Chapter 15.

Fig. 12–12. The weft passes through the bugle beads from one motif to another.

To make a choker, for instance, start with a medallion design. Judge how long the choker should be, then measure this length on the warp, starting from the knot on the reverse side of the Formica and adding a little more to allow for casting-off. First you weave over eight warp threads until a medallion is formed. Then divide the weave into two bands, which

13. Which beads to use

It is advisable to begin by using beads of the same size (fig. 13–1). First draw the pattern on squared paper. From this you can decide whether the warp should be visible, what colour it should be, and which kind of thread to use for the weft. Even small children can learn to weave with beads of the same size.

Working with children

Bead-work with children has a threefold purpose:

(1) to develop their manual skills (the child learns to pick the bead up and put it down again, then later to weave a needle and thread through warp and weft);

(2) to teach them to count, since counting is a basic component of weaving (the child learns to count up to certain numbers, to respect these amounts, and then to count out fresh amounts of beads); and

(3) to teach them the basic principles of language (the child learns to use concepts like: underneath, above, next, before, behind, there and back, which can be explained visually while weaving beads).

If you are working with children, you should use beads that are large, colourful, easy to pick up, and which have a very large hole. Children cannot handle very small beads because they are difficult to pick up, whereas beads that are too large are difficult to weave into a pattern, and they make a weave appear untidy. The

Fig. 13–1. Part of a belt made with beads of the same size. It consists of a wide pattern in the centre which gradually narrows until it joins the rest of the belt, which is made of wool.

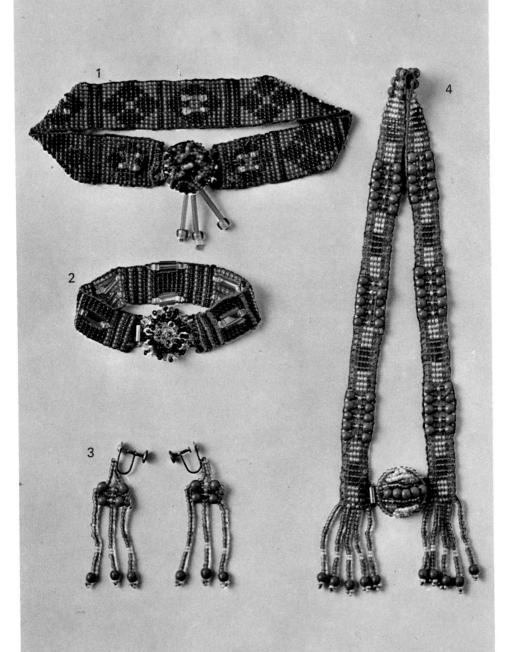

Opposite.
Colour Plate 2. 1. Choker. 2. Bracelet.
3. Earrings. 4. Necklace.
These illustrations show clearly how the
various articles were made. Patterns for the
choker and the bracelet were drawn on graph
paper. The ends of the choker were finished-
off with about $\frac{1}{4}$ in. (6 mm.) of plain
weaving, which was then turned back and
sewn to the bead-work. The metal clasp was
attached afterwards to these sections of
plain weaving. The necklace was made by
weaving a straight band, the ends of which
were turned into strings of beads, and the
metal clasp was sewn on to the warp threads
on the sides of the band.

Colour Plate 3. Purple weave. This piece of
work has been woven on a frame with nails.
First a string warp was set up; then a finer
warp with threaded beads was set up over
the first one. Surfaces and bands in a range
of purples and pinks were woven in a
variety of techniques, and beads were added
by passing the weft through the thinner
warp. When the weave was finished it was
removed from the frame, and the warp was
unravelled at the foot.

beads that the Africans once used as currency are ideal for children. These beads used to be made in Italy, but now they are made in Czechoslovakia (fig. 13–2). They are about $\frac{1}{4}$ in. (6 mm.) in diameter, and they have a band about $\frac{1}{12}$ in. (2 mm.) wide around them. They are often sold specifically as children's beads.

When teaching very young children 5–6 years) to weave, begin with numbers one to five, and repeat these numbers

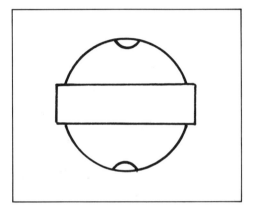

Fig. 13–2. Children's bead.

Fig. 13–3. 1 and 2. Patterns with children's beads.

often. For example, you can start by placing a little box or bowl of beads in front of the children. From this they can choose one bead, which will have a particular colour — red, for example. Now ask them to put four red beads in a group, then to make five groups of four beads. Next, they can choose another colour from the bowl or box — say, white. Now they can put five white beads together and form four groups of five beads. After the children have done this they will be able to count how many red and white beads there are altogether. They will then discover that there are as many white beads as there are red ones.

After the children have counted the red and white beads they are ready to go a step further. The beads are now lying in front of the children in two groups of different colours. (The exercise is still limited to numbers from one to five; one, four, and five have already been mentioned.) Ask them to form a row of three

Opposite.
Fig. 13–4. 1 and 2. Necklaces. Both pieces of work have a rather complicated structure that uses beads of different sizes to create open and closed sections. Both necklaces are fastened with clasps; the clasp in photograph 2 is itself decorated with beads.

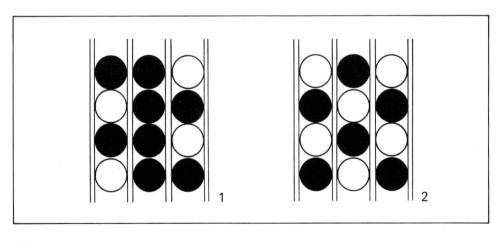

1

2

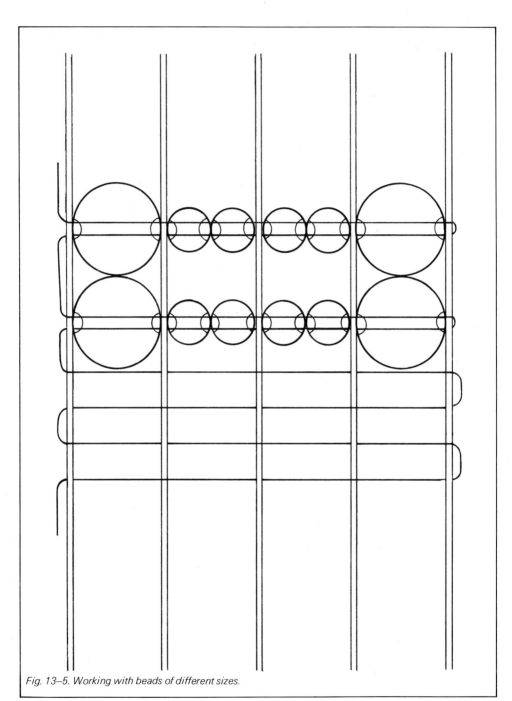

Fig. 13–5. Working with beads of different sizes.

Page 53.
Fig. 13–6. Head-band. The front and back were woven separately with beads of different sizes. The bands are broadest toward the middle, narrowing off toward the ends. The bands were removed from the frame after weaving, and the warp threads of the back part were slipped through the last woven row of beads on the front part to hang down to the left of the face. The warp threads of the front part hang to the right of the face. Both these groups of hanging warp threads were then strung with beads, creating a highly decorative effect when the head moves.

beads, choosing at random from the two groups of beads in front of them. Then ask them to form another row of three beads underneath the first one, but with the colours arranged in a different order. For example, if the first row was red-white-red, the second row can be white-red-white, etc. (fig. 13–3). These two rows will be repeated constantly in the weaving, forming a simple pattern.

This exercise should be well within the capacities of the children, but since the process of weaving itself demands a certain amount of concentration, the pattern should be kept relatively simple. Older children can master the craft of weaving in this way, and later they can work with more complicated patterns which can first be laid out on the table.

Small children cannot be expected to set up the warp on the Formica, so you should set up four threads on it and ask the children to count them. Then you ask them to count the spaces between the threads; there are three. You can point out that three beads will eventually be positioned in these spaces. Weave a single row to show how the beads are first threaded on the needle and then pushed into the spaces between the warp threads from underneath; now let the children pull the needle and thread through while securing the beads by holding them from underneath. Next the children can thread the weft back through the same beads and weave the second

row of three beads, followed by a repeat of the first. It may be necessary to demonstrate the process several times, but once the children have understood they will find it quite easy. Naturally, an adult will have to do the finishing-off, but the children will have done the actual weaving.

Working with bead-units

Weaving with beads of varying sizes is more difficult, but it also offers more possibilities. You can use large and small beads together, for instance, two rows of small beads, followed by two rows of large beads, etc. Large and small beads can also be used next to each other in the same row. You must make sure, however, that the larger beads lie along the outer warp threads which hold the whole weave together. The smaller beads should be positioned in the centre of the pattern, creating a lace-like effect, since they do not fill up the weave completely (fig. 13–4).

If the loose weave needs to be filled up, you can do it as follows: thread a large bead, followed by some small ones, then another large one, on to the needle. Weave this row in between the warp threads; next thread on another row made up entirely of small beads, and pass it underneath the warp to fill up any remaining space. Pass the thread back through these beads, thereby filling up the whole weave. Another possibility is to weave two small beads into the spaces in the warp which would otherwise be occupied by one large bead (fig. 13–5).

This seems to contradict the rule that you should always have one bead between two warp threads, since you now have two beads. You should now begin to think in terms of bead-units: only one bead-unit can lie between two warp threads. These bead-units are interchangeable; for instance, you can have two small beads on one row, followed by one large bead on the next row (fig. 13–5).

14. Plain weaving with beads

Both weft and warp can play a part in the final weave (fig. 14–1). The warp does not pass through any of the beads unless you have specifically threaded some beads on to it to lie lengthways in the weave, but all sorts of variations are possible with the weft. You can choose a thread for the weft which is the same colour as the warp, and weave sections with the thread alone in between sections of bead-weaving. There is no need to weave the weft through all the warp threads; you can weave through just a few and back again. If a similar piece of weaving is needed on the other side of the article, take a new length of weft and repeat the same pattern. It is not possible to weave both sides at once with the same weft. In fig. 14–1 the middle part of the warp has been left unwoven; it is here that the bead-weaving can be done, thus creating a complete weave in which the bead-weaving is bordered by two sections of plain weaving. Alternatively you may have borders of bead-weaving with plain weaving in the centre.

The weft is usually thinner than the warp, but the same thread can be used for both. (Make sure that the thread can be passed at least twice through the hole of the bead.) You will soon notice that this technique (combining plain weaving with bead-weaving) involves quite a lot of casting-on and -off, since it is often impossible to weave different sections with the same length of thread. It is very difficult to indicate in advance how to deal with this problem; as in all craft work, you should find out which method you prefer by experimenting. It is very important to examine the characteristics of the materials you are going to use before starting to work. Each problem requires a fresh solution, which is one reason why working with different techniques simultaneously is so fascinating.

Page 56.
Fig. 14–1. Detail of a wall ornament. The uppermost part was braided in string and then divided into smaller braids and loose beads, between which a number of small sticks were slipped. At the bottom the strings were drawn together again in braid-work. The centre parts were woven, and the edges were decorated with beads.

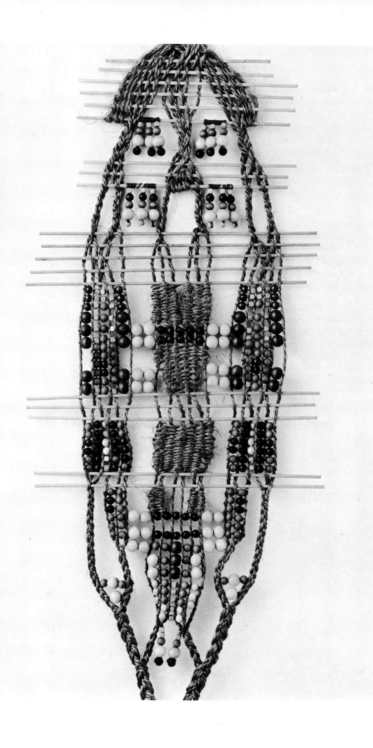

15. Bead-weaving in combination with other techniques

Macramé

As mentioned in Chapter 12, when the threads of the warp are knotted in bunches behind the loom it is possible to have a much longer length of thread at your disposal. If you want to add some macramé knotting in between the sections

Fig. 15–1. Finishing-off with macramé.

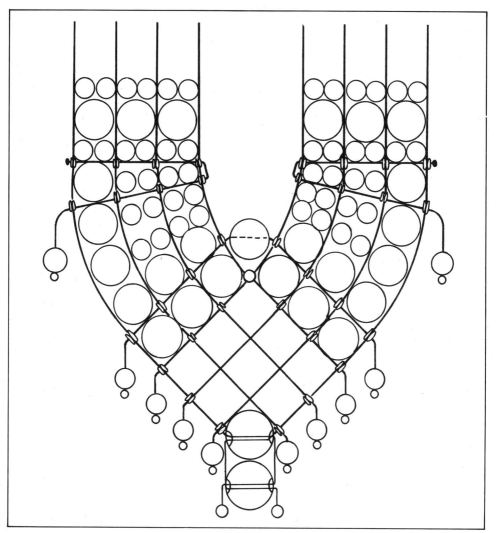

Fig. 15–2. Necklace. The necklace itself is
simply threaded. The emphasis is on the loose
woven sections which hang from it, in which
long round bugle beads were incorporated.
The warp threads of the hanging sections
were simply knotted to the thread of the
neck section.

of bead-weaving you must make sure that there is enough thread to spare, since a knot takes up a lot of thread. Make a rough sketch of the work in advance, indicating the approximate position of the knots, so that you can estimate roughly how much thread is required. If you are using only simple knots such as the flat knot or the lark's head, you can count on using six and a half times the length of the warp. The length needed for the actual bead-weave is easily calculated on the basis of the length of the beads to be used.

Start the work in the middle of the concave side of the Formica, though this section may eventually form the middle or even one of the ends of the final article. The knots containing the reserve thread now lie underneath the Formica in the middle of the convex side (fig. 12–5). In this way there is the same length of thread on either side of the starting point of your work. If the weave is to .be finished-off with knot-work, then the threads can either be left hanging as they are or unravelled.

First weave a section with beads, then let out the knots at the back of the Formica a little, and start to work on the macramé section, with or without beads. If you use a strong warp like yarn you can let the knots stand by themselves without adding any beads between them. This method allows the two techniques to set each other off to the best advantage. In any case, knotted yarn does give a bead-like effect.

Once again you can see that a warp which is knotted behind the loom offers more possibilities than one which is simply wound continuously round it. The weave can be unknotted before it is finished to see what kind of effect it makes, and you do not have to repeat one fixed pattern after another. You may also start weaving a running pattern some distance from one end of the warp and finish it off some distance from the other end, thus allowing room to widen the finished piece of work. This effect can be accentuated by making the threads into tassels (fig. 15–2).

When a finished weave has to be fastened at the back, such as a necklace (colour plate 2), you can incorporate a clasp decorated with beads similar to those used in the rest of the weave.

Bead-threading

Bead-weaving and bead-threading can also be combined. In a pattern which has a fairly small number of warp threads, you can use them to make ornamental thread-work between the woven sections. When you have finished the threading, knot the warp threads at the back of the Formica again, and start the weaving. You can begin somewhere in the middle of the design, perhaps taking the knot behind the Formica as the limit of the weave. The motif at the end of the work can be formed by bead-weaving and the lengths of thread left over threaded with more beads so that the entire pattern of the weave is filled out (fig. 15–3).

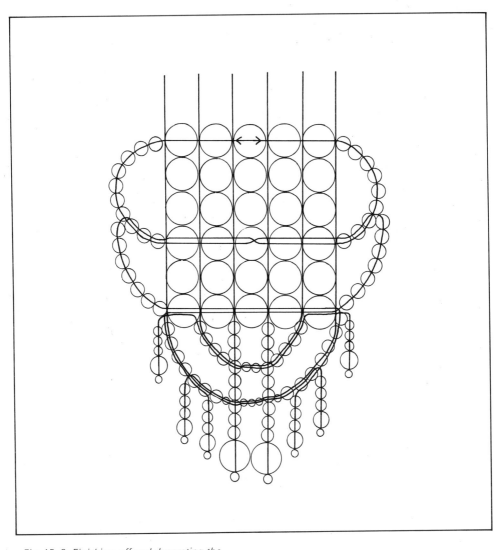

Fig. 15–3. Finishing-off and decorating the
warp threads.

60

16. Finishing-off in bead-weaving

It is essential to have enough thread to finish the weave off properly. If the warp has been set up simply by winding it round the Formica, then at least 6 in. (15 cm.) must be left at the end for finishing-off. Rather less is needed at the beginning, about 4 in. (10 cm.). In all you should allow about 10 in. (25 cm.) of unwoven warp, and you should not cut the thread until after you have made sure that the requisite lengths have been retained (fig. 16–1).

Fig. 16–1. Cutting the warp.

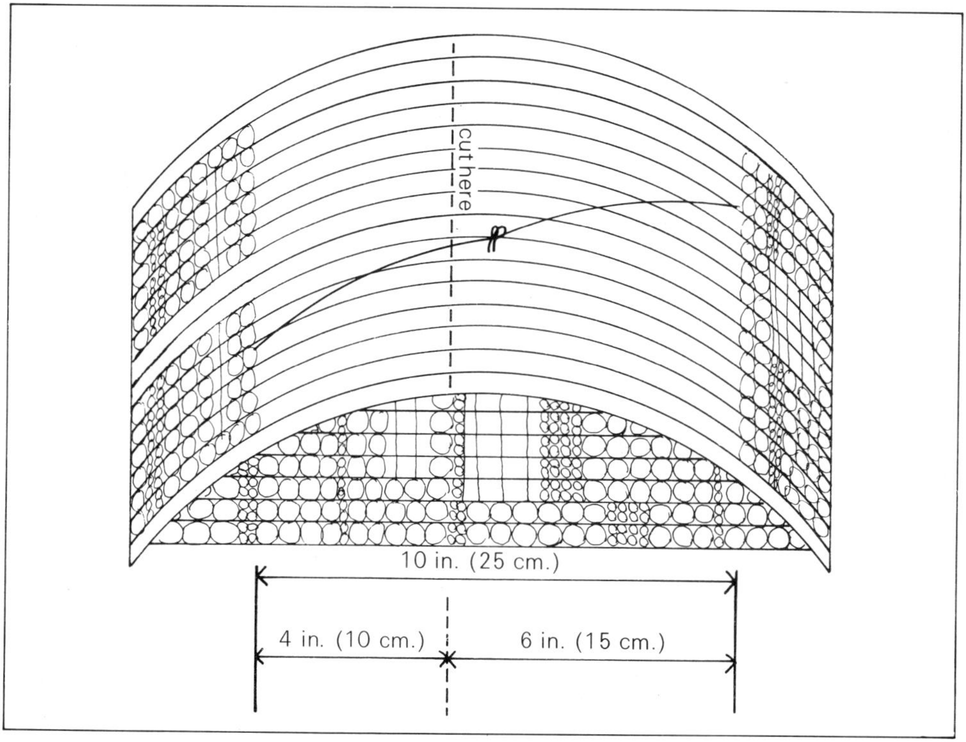

cut here

10 in. (25 cm.)

4 in. (10 cm.)   6 in. (15 cm.)

Fig. 16–2. Necklaces. All the necklaces were
made with beads of the same size. First a
medallion was woven with beads of various
colours, then the weave was divided into
two separate bands to form the section
which goes round the neck. The finishing-off
is different in each necklace:
1. The strings of beads at the foot were made
into bows, and the beads on either side of
the medallion were sewn on with loop
stitches. 2. Beads were strung along two of
the hanging threads, while the remainder
were combined to form a central ornament.
3. Bow-shaped and hanging strings of beads
were combined.

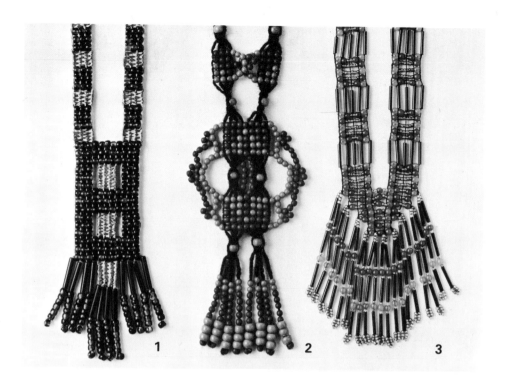

Fig. 16–3. Various ways of finishing-off:
1. The central sections are in plain weave, and surrounding parts in bead-weave. The weave was finished-off with bugle beads and round beads similar to those in the main part of the necklace. The strings of beads hanging from the necklace have different lengths. 2. This necklace shows how bead-weaving, macramé, and bead-threading can be combined. The weaving was started at one end of a Formica loom; after the first section of bead-weave the warp was undone, and macramé knots and threaded beads were added. The warp was then put back on the loom and the bead-weaving continued. When the medallion section was finished the warp was divided in two parts, which were woven and knotted separately. Then bow-shaped strings of beads were added to the medallion to give it a rounded appearance.

The ends were finished-off with macramé knotting, ending in strings of beads. The knots were secured with glue because the warp was quite thick. 3. The warp was threaded with bugle beads. The medallion section was started with four warp threads, and gradually more and more threads and beads of different sizes were added to create a slanting effect. Then the warp was divided into two parts, which were woven separately. Bugle beads were slipped along the warp threads in between the sections of bead-weaving to produce variations in the design. The lace effect in the bead-weaving was created by placing larger beads on the outside and filling up the centre with smaller ones. Because the warp was so thin it was doubled, thus producing a large number of threads at the bottom of the necklace, which were then strung with rows of beads.

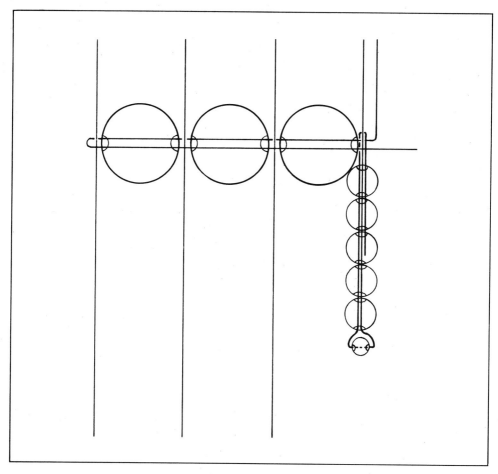

Fig. 16–4. Finishing-off a string of beads.

Colour Plate 4. Weaving on a wooden frame. A frame with nails on the underside was assembled, then the warp was set up with irregular spaces between different threads to produce a very open effect. A number of coloured threads and beads were then woven freely into the warp. When this weave is hung it projects shadows on to the surface behind it.

The easiest way to finish-off is to thread a number of beads on to each warp thread. One or more of the end beads can be used as stop beads (fig. 16–4), by taking the thread through them again, slipping it over the last weft thread, and passing it yet again through a few of the beads threaded on the warp (fig. 16–4).

If you finish-off in this way the strings of beads will always hang extremely well. But the warp thread should not be too thick, because it has to pass at least three times through some of the beads (fig. 16–4).

If you have used a thick warp, then you must finish-off in another way. The easiest alternatives are to use either larger beads in the same colour as those in the weave, or macramé, finishing-off with another bead or a knot. The strands which are left hanging can be of different lengths, according to what suits the work best.

Another way to finish-off is to thread beads on to the warp and then to fashion these into a bow which will hang at the ends of the work. Other warp threads can be used to form strings of beads to hang between those which have been made into bows (fig. 13–4).

To finish-off at the top of a choker (or whatever the work may be), divide the warp threads into two groups and insert a pencil between them (fig. 16–5). (This is only possible with an even number of warp threads. If there is an uneven number of threads, separate the middle thread, and deal with it separately by slipping it back through the beads.) Half of the warp threads are wound round the pencil, while the rest are pushed aside for the moment. With a separate length of thread (such as very thin sewing thread) catch up the loop formed by the warp threads round the pencil. These threads can then be secured with a spot of glue. If the warp threads are long enough there is no need to introduce a new thread; one of the warp threads can catch up the others. When all the warp threads have been caught up in this way, bend a hook out of a metal strip (or buy one), and sew it on to one of the loops formed by the warp threads. This method of finishing-off can be done by anyone quite easily (fig. 16–5).

Another method is to decorate a clasp with beads and to attach the warp

Fig. 16–5. Finishing-off the threads at the end of a loop.

threads to it. In this case the work is not fastened with a simple hook passing through a loop, but with a device made up of two parts. Such clasps are on sale everywhere and can easily be decorated with beads. You should use beads similar to those which have already been used in the main part of the weave (fig. 13–4).

17. Bead-weaving on another loom

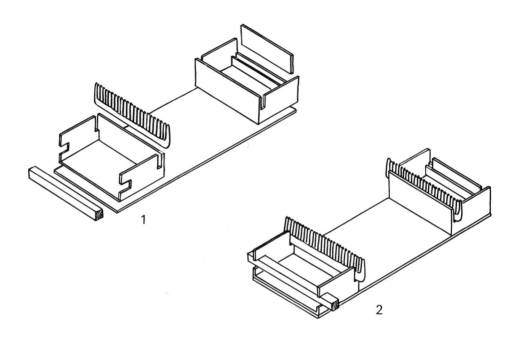

Fig. 17–1.

Constructing the loom

You can make an excellent and handsome bead-loom from a small but deep cigar-box, two even-toothed plastic or metal pocket combs 6 in. (15 cm.) long, a board, and some small pieces of wood.

Saw the box in half and stick the two halves back to back on to a board with contact glue, about 10 in. (25 cm.) from each other. This will allow room for your hands to move while you are weaving. Then cut a groove in the side edges of both halves. Set the combs in the grooves to keep the warp threads separate while you are weaving. In the back side of one half cut a notch for a square piece of

Fig. 17–2. A bead-loom can be assembled
from a cigar-box cut in half, a board, two
pocket combs, and some small pieces of
wood.

Fig. 17–3.

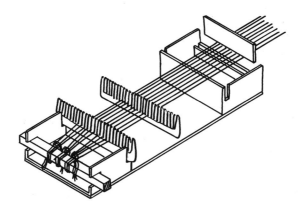

wood, which should be slightly longer than the width of the box. The warp thread will be wound round this stick so that it will not slip while you are weaving.

The warp thread must be stretched and fastened to the other half of the box. The basic idea is to press the warp down into a slot, where it is held in place by a piece of cigar-box wood. The tension will be greater if you fold a small piece of cardboard round the piece of wood.

Rub the sides and edges of the loom carefully with sandpaper so that you will not catch the threads while you work.

Setting up the warp

You will remember that the warp is the long thread in weaving, and the weft is the weaving thread which goes across. The width of the weft depends on the number of warp threads you set up, just as the length depends on the length of the warp threads. Since the beads lie between the warp threads, you must put one more thread on the loom than the number of beads in the row. To strengthen the piece of woven fabric, double some of the threads at the edges.

You should use strong thread for the warp: white crochet yarn D.M.C. no. 100, nylon, or polyester thread for small beads, and even stronger yarn for larger beads. White thread generally looks most natural and inconspicuous for the warp, although you can use coloured yarn if you want the warp to stand out in the design. Stretch each thread singly. To make sure that they are all the same length, you can wind them round the back of a chair, a large book, or a file.

Knot the warp round the squared stick in groups of five to fifteen threads. If you use a comb 6 in. (15 cm.) wide you can get at least eighty beads across the whole width. Separate the warp threads between the teeth of the comb, stretch the warp tight in the slot at the other end of the loom, and you are ready to start weaving.

If you want to make a long piece of bead-work on this loom you can loosen the warp threads from the slot after you have woven a bit and roll the woven piece round the squared stick, as shown in fig. 17–4. When you have tautened the warp threads again you can carry on weaving from where you stopped. After you have rolled up the woven piece in this way you will not need the comb any longer.

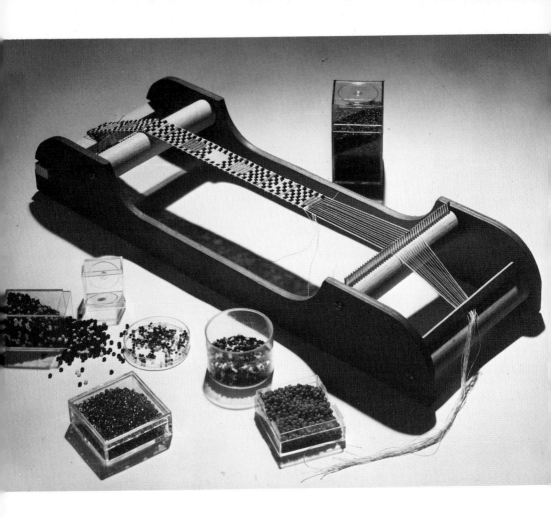

Fig. 17–4. A ready-made loom which can be assembled and dismantled at home. The bead-weaving on the loom is long enough to wind round the stick holding the warp at the back. The comb in the roller has been turned downwards, since there is no longer any need for it. The transparent plastic boxes store the beads so that you can find the right size or colour easily. It is impractical to have more than two different sizes or colours of beads in one box.

Weaving

Before you start weaving, remember that both the needle and the weft thread must be able to pass at least two or three times through the holes of the beads. A no. 10 needle is recommended, and you should rub the weft with wax.

Beginners are advised to start by weaving a narrow strip with a repeating pattern. On a practice piece like this you can see whether the colours of the pattern stand out sufficiently from the background. To start the weaving, knot the weft thread to the left-hand warp thread, and leave the end hanging. Thread the beads on to the weft thread and press the row of beads up under the warp with your fingers so that the beads separate between the warp threads. Then pass the weft thread through the beads, going over the warp thread and back to the beginning of the row. Sew into the preceding row of beads occasionally so that the whole piece will be firm.

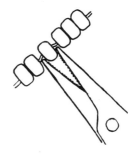

After you have woven four or five rows thread the loose weft thread at the beginning over these rows, and make a small, firm edge by darning into the empty warp thread. Then simply continue weaving as before.

If you want to include bugle beads in the web wait until you have already woven five or six rows in the ordinary way. You will have to push the bugle beads on to the warp threads, so you will need to loosen them from the slot. As the edges of these beads can be quite sharp, it is practical to put one round bead on the warp before and after each bugle bead. These two round beads can add to the effect of the pattern if you choose a different colour for them. Before you continue weaving, stretch the warp threads tightly in the slot again.

Fig. 17–5.

When you have finished the weaving completely, weave up and down with the end of the weft thread as you did at the beginning. Knot the warp threads together in pairs. (These last knots are necessary only if you are weaving a fairly large piece of bead-work.) Turn all the warp threads under and sew them securely into the back of the work.

If you have mistakenly put too many beads on to the thread while weaving, it is easier to shatter them with a flat-headed pair of pliers than to unthread all the beads. Put the pliers round the holes of the beads so that there is no danger of the cutting edge breaking the thread.

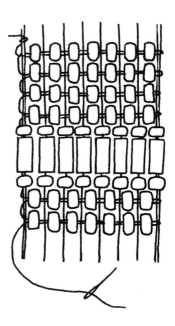

Fig. 17–6.

Fig. 17–7. These necklaces were woven on a bead-loom. The long bugle beads were drawn on to the warp threads, and the other beads were woven out round them. The necklace in photograph 1 has grey, orange, and dark blue round beads, and transparent green bugle beads. The necklace in photograph 2 has round beads of lavender and dark red, while the bugle beads are gold.

18. Practical pattern ideas

Strips for belts and head-bands

You can make a simple ground by weaving narrow borders five beads wide. A single bead border can be varied just by changing the colours round, as in fig. 18–1. Narrow borders of five beads like this can be put to an endless number of uses. For example, you can make a ribbon for your spectacles so that you always know where they are. Borders six to fifteen beads across are suitable for head-bands. The length of the weft will vary according to the individual. The strip of beads is sewn on to thin leather, and the ends are folded back to make two open loops which are then held together by a couple of narrow strips of leather tied in a knot. Fig. 18–2 shows how the same fastening technique can be used for belts.

You can sew an attractive belt out of chamois leather folded round a length of stiff ribbon and sewn together with small stitches on the reverse side. On top of this you can sew small bead motifs like those shown in the diagrams in fig. 18–11.

The photographs and diagrams in fig. 18–3 are for head-bands of different widths. All are woven on a loom and lined with a piece of thin glove leather.

Bead jewelry mounted on leather

The previous section described ribbons woven completely from beads, but leather ribbons can be used as well, since leather and glass beads make an excellent combination.

Fig. 18–4, photograph 1 shows a pendant of an 'assembly of elephants', which is composed of three elephant pictures woven separately, then sewn together and mounted on a backing of flannel, thin cardboard, and leather. The string of natural-coloured leather is not just a strip round the neck but an integral part of the whole pendant.

The pattern for the elephant design is shown in fig. 18–5, diagram 1. The elephant is grey with an orange saddle

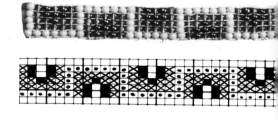

Fig. 18–1.

rug on a pink background. The borders and the small chains on the leather are dark blue and white.

The geometric pendant in fig. 18–4, photograph 2 has a white bead background and pointed patterns alternating black and red. The squares inside the points are blue and yellow. Red and white beads are sewn up the folded strip of black leather. The pattern for this is given in fig. 18–5, diagram 2.

The pendant with the repeated pattern in fig. 18–4, photograph 3 is made as a whole piece. The patterns have orange, turquoise, blue, and red backgrounds, all with white outlines. The loops of the fringe are red under the blue panel with the lowest bead blue, and blue with a red tip under the red panel. The double leather ribbon is natural-coloured and completely free from decoration. The pattern for this pendant is in fig. 18–5, diagram 3.

Woven necklaces

Beginning weavers should start with something very simple, like the bead necklace with diagonal stripes shown in fig. 18–6, photograph 1, which is 18 in. (45 cm.) long.

This necklace has a pale purple background with a brightly coloured diagonal pattern. The web should be nineteen beads wide, or twenty-four warp threads (about 24 in. (60 cm.) long) on the loom, since the two outer threads are tripled to make the edges of the woven piece stronger. (Note that each row should have an uneven number of beads so that the pattern will work out symmetrically.)

Weave twenty-two rows, then divide the web into two ribbons, each five beads wide. Keep the centre warp threads empty since you must continue weaving until the ribbons reach the required length. Keep the same background colour for the ribbons, and repeat the colours you have used in the stripes of the medallion as small separate motifs.

When you have finished the weaving sew the bead ribbons together carefully at the back of the neck by darning the warp threads backwards and forwards through nine or ten rows of beads.

Knot the empty warp threads from the centre together in pairs and sew them into the medallion. Mount the medallion as described in Chapter 8. Then sew loops, each consisting of twelve pale purple beads, into the sides. The loops are interconnected by groups of six beads in the colours of the diagonal stripes.

The large pendant in fig. 18–6, photograph 2, for which you will find the pattern in fig. 18–8, diagram 1, is composed of a flower motif on a white background. The petals are turquoise and dark blue with orange centres. The stylized stalks are grass green. The diamond in the centre of the medallion is made of red, turquoise, and dark blue beads. The ribbon round the neck is in crosswise stripes of white, turquoise, and dark blue.

The little necklace with three hearts in

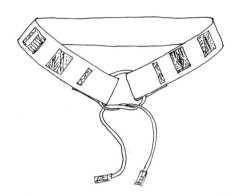

Fig. 18–2.

Opposite.
Fig. 18–3.

fig. 18–7, photograph 2 is fastened at the neck with a screw fitting. To make this, set up the warp for twenty-one beads, begin by weaving the first row with nine beads in the middle of the warp, and add one bead on each side of every row until there are twenty-one beads. Weave eight rows on all of these beads, and then decrease one bead on each side until there are nine beads. Continue weaving on two narrow ribbons, each nineteen rows long. Then take the work off the loom. Knot the warp threads in the ribbons and continue to the required length with two double chains, then sew in the screw fastening.

The large necklace with fringes on the bottom shown in fig. 18–7, photograph 1 has a background of white beads and black and orange beads for the pattern. When finished the necklace is 19 in. (47 cm.) long, and the fringes are $1\frac{1}{8}$ in. (3 cm.) long.

For the weaving set up thirty-four warp threads about 26 in. (65 cm.) long, and triple the outer threads for strength, which amounts to thirty-eight threads altogether.

Fig. 18–4. Pendants in different shapes and
patterns.

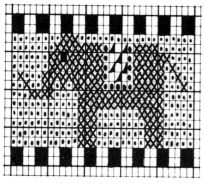

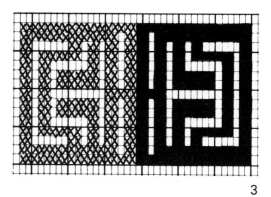

1

3

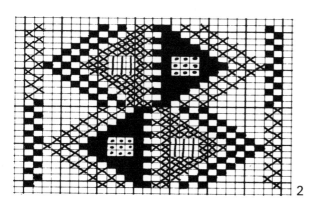

2

Fig. 18–5. Motif diagrams for bead bracelets and other bead jewelry.

Start weaving across the wide part of the necklace with thirty-two beads across for thirty-two rows. When you have woven these rows, divide the necklace in to two long ribbons with eleven beads in each row. The remaining warp threads at the centre can be knotted together as described above. Sew the excess warp into the weft.

Repeat the triangular pattern in the two ribbons six times, then decrease to nine beads in each row. The extra warp threads can be taken up gradually as weft threads as they become free.

Continue weaving in stripes with these nine beads for about 1 in. (2·5 cm.), then decrease again and make another piece 1 in. (2·5 cm.) long with seven beads. The last and narrowest piece is five beads wide and about 7 in. (18 cm.) long.

When the ribbons are done finish them off in the usual way, and mount the bead-work. Trim the necklace by sewing a fringe border on to the bottom.

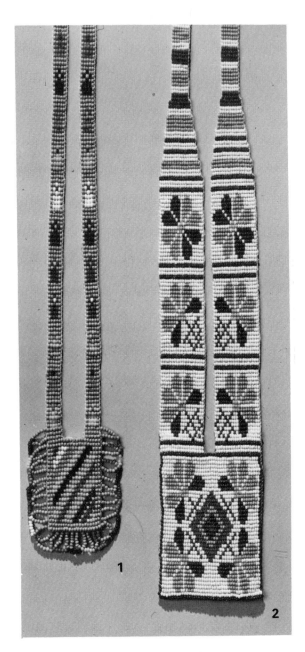

Fig. 18–6.

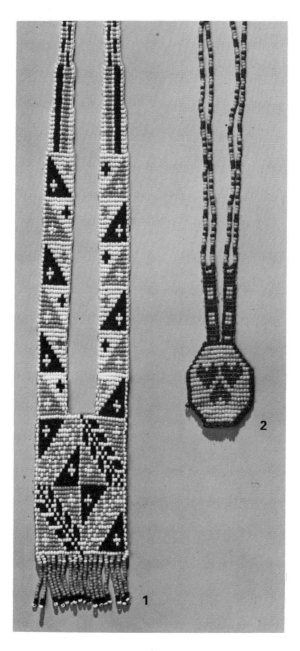

Fig. 18–7.

Fig. 18–8. 1 and 2. Diagrams for the pendant and the upper part of the right-hand necklace in fig. 18–6. 3 and 4. Diagrams for the pendant and the upper part of the left-hand necklace in fig. 18–7.

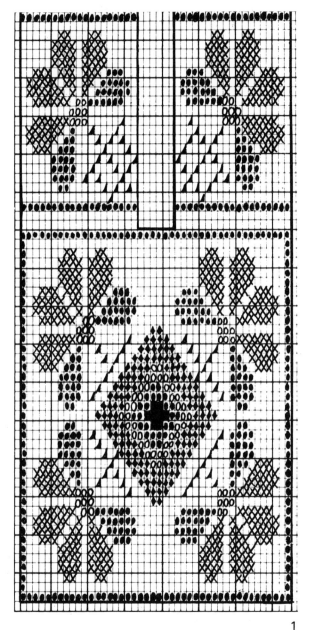

1

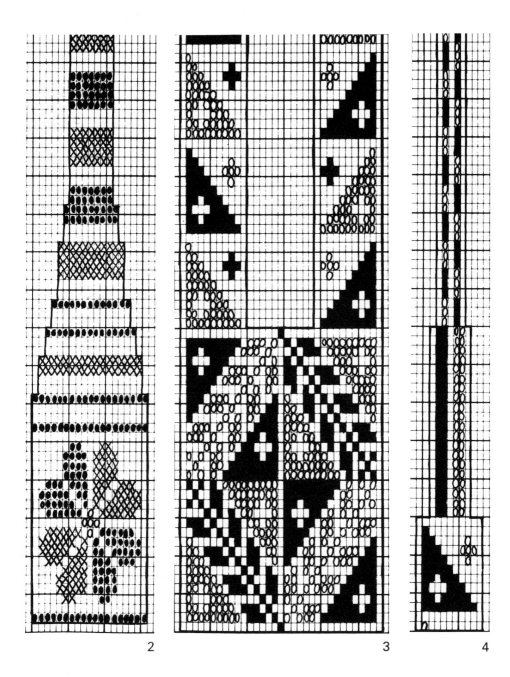

2   3   4

A woven bead bracelet

For the bracelet to fit easily, the actual woven work should be $\frac{3}{8}$ in. (1 cm.) larger than the measurement round the widest part of the hand. This may vary from about 8–10 in. (19–25 cm.)

Use a repeating bead pattern to your taste, but if you cannot fit in a complete number of repeats you can always weave another small variation to finish it off. There are several pattern instructions in the diagrams in fig. 18–11, though you can easily design an original pattern yourself.

When you have taken the web off the loom knot all the long warp threads together in pairs to keep the beads firmly in place. Form the bead-work into a circle and sew in and out of the beads in the first and last rows where you have made the knots. Finish-off by sewing small stitches backwards and forwards over the loose thread ends on the back so that the bracelet feels firm. This stitching should be as invisible as possible. Fig. 18–10, photograph 1 shows the first stages in making the bracelet.

Next cut a stiff piece of ribbon to fit. Stick this together with Sellotape to form a ring. Fit the stiff ribbon inside the bead-work as in fig. 18–10, photograph 2. Put another piece of stiff ribbon inside to serve as an exact cutting pattern for a piece of thin leather lining.

Cut a double width of leather since it should fit round both ribbon rings.

Sew the piece of leather together on the reverse side to form a circle. Then place it inside the ribbon rings, turn it inside-out, and tack all the layers together with large stitches along the length of the bracelet. Push the edges of the bead-work down over the leather, and sew them together with fine stitches along the top and bottom of the bracelet. Use double sewing silk in the colour of the leather for this.

Smooth over the stitching on the leather with the eyes of your scissors so that it lies flat and feels comfortable.

Fig. 18–9.

Opposite.
Fig. 18–10. 1. The first stages in bead-weaving a bracelet. 2. Stiff ribbon and leather cut to double width and fitted inside the bead-work. 3. Finished bracelets.

You can also make napkin rings this way. The bird pattern in fig. 18–11 was designed especially for this purpose.

Bags and purses

A colourful piece of bead-work will stand out on an evening bag and, since it wears so well, on an everyday shoulder bag as well.

One or more borders on the flap of an envelope-shaped leather bag make a lock unnecessary because the weight of the beads will hold the flap down.

A drawstring bag made of chamois with a round, oval, or cornered base will stand endless washings even with a bead motif.

For small, modest presents you might consider making a little leather case for car keys or covering a large matchbox with a piece of leather on which you have sewn a woven bead motif. Something like this will have a long life even if transferred to a new box.

83

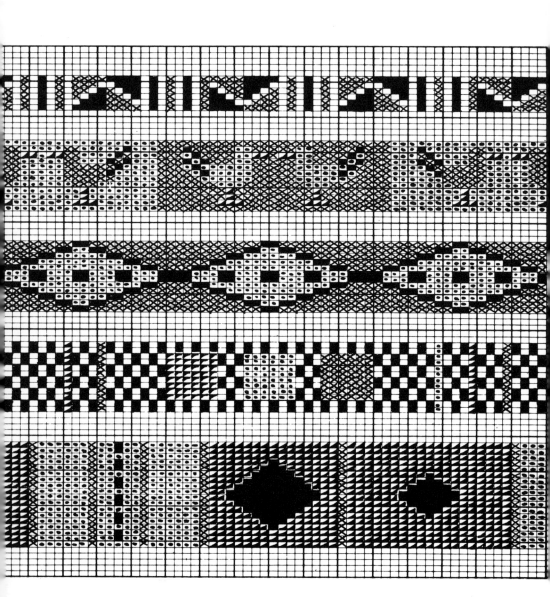

Fig. 18–11. Motif diagrams for bead bracelets
or other woven bands.

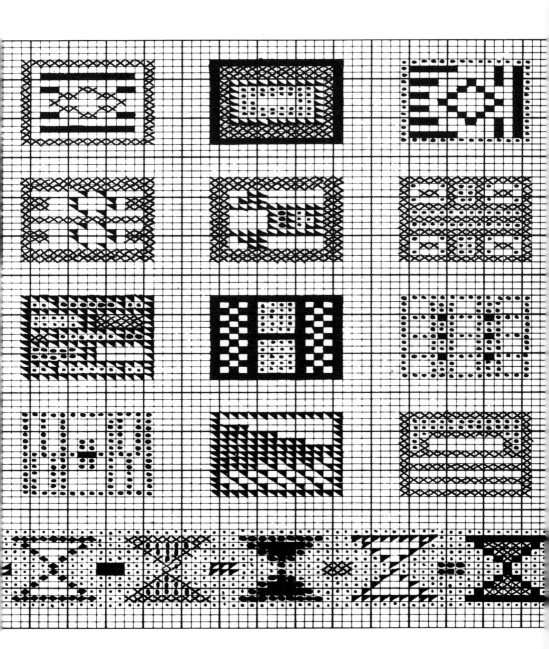

Fig. 18–12. Leather purse decorated with beads. The top section is slit so that the purse can be slipped on a belt.

Fig. 18–14. Suede handbag with a large woven bead panel. The background is white, with alternating patterns in strong and pastel colours. The suede itself is grey.

Fig. 18–13. Diagram for the purse illustrated in fig. 18–12.

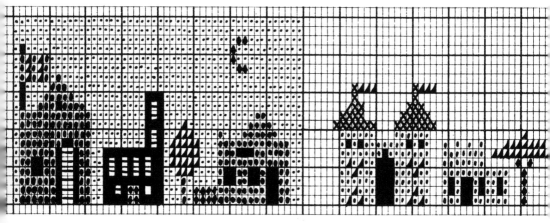

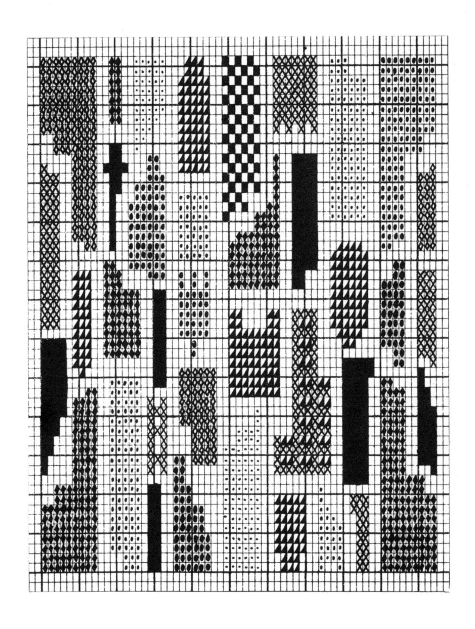

Fig. 18–15. Pattern diagram for the bag
shown in fig. 18–14.

19. Weaving on round and square frames

There are a number of ways to produce larger articles either in bead-weave alone or combined with plain weave.

Round frames

For round weaving the warp must be set up in a series of spokes. You can make a number of indentations at regular intervals round the circumference of a round piece of cardboard, and then attach the warp threads as shown in fig. 19–1, always making sure that the beginning is secure.

You can also hammer in a number of small nails round the edge of a disk-shaped piece of wood (strong plywood, for instance), as shown in fig. 19–2. The warp thread is carried from one nail to the nail opposite, then on to the next nail round the circumference.

The easiest method, however, is to set up the warp on a metal ring. This ring can remain in the finished article, whereas cardboard or wood generally must be removed. The thread is attached at some point along the ring and taken across to the opposite point on the circumference; a number of loop stitches are then made round the ring to determine the distance between the warp threads. The thread is then taken back across the ring, and a further set of loop stitches is made. This process is repeated until the whole area enclosed by the ring is criss-crossed by the warp threads (fig. 19–3). This process will leave much of the circumference of the ring empty. This space can also be covered with loop stitches, but you should leave this until the weave is completed because you can still adjust the warp threads round the ring while the space is left free, which is very useful if any variation in the distances between them is required. Set up the warp with the thread wound up in a little ball, since you will need too much thread to carry on a needle; it is always much easier to work with a ball of wool than with a needle and thread.

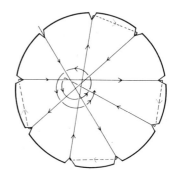

Fig. 19–1. Setting up the warp threads on a round piece of cardboard.

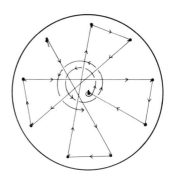

Fig. 19–2. Setting up the warp threads on a disk of wood with nails.

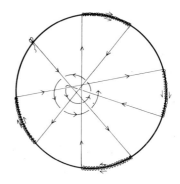

Fig. 19–3. Setting up the warp threads on a round metal ring.

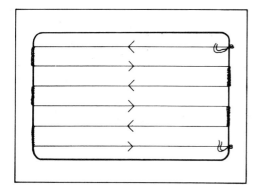

Fig. 19–4. Setting up the warp threads on a square frame.

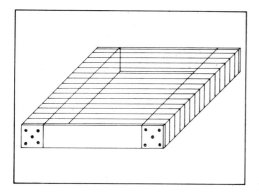

Fig. 19–5. Setting up the warp threads on a home-made frame.

When working with round frames, whether weaving ready-made patterns or your own designs, the problem of the distance between each warp thread must be confronted. Remember that the threads are farther apart along the circumference than they are at the centre.

To make the weft, pass a double thickness of thread twice round the frame, thus forming a thicker section in the weave so that the threads will be secure enough to begin weaving. It is never possible to weave directly in the centre since the warp threads lie on top of each other, but make sure that you have an even number of warp threads so that the under and over patterns of the weft match. In the round weave in fig. 19–6, some of the weft threads do not pass completely round the circle; certain areas of colour can reach only part of the way round the design. Parts of the pattern where the weft has been repeatedly woven to and fro have been left completely open.

Beads can be incorporated in the finished design by threading them on the weft, but they must be suited to the distance between the warp threads. Beads which are too large to fit between the threads will make the work bulge unpleasantly, whereas beads which are too small will slip along the weft too easily, spoiling the effect of the finished weave. Larger beads will obviously be needed the closer the weft gets to the circumference, since the warp threads are farther apart here than in the centre. This asymmetry, however, can be exploited to create interesting star shapes which, together with sections of plain weaving, form an exciting structure of alternating coloured areas.

It is advisable to use relatively strong thread round the edges of the pattern where the warp threads are the greatest distance apart and thinner thread towards the centre. If thin thread is used through-out, it may begin to pull in towards the centre, especially if the frame is removed afterwards, and the finished weave will not lie flat. This is not as serious when the frame remains in the work, since the warp threads will then be kept taut in any case (fig. 19–6).

Square frames

To set up the warp on a square metal frame, follow exactly the same process as with a round frame: first secure the warp by knotting it to the side of the frame; then bring it over to the opposite side, and loop it round the frame to determine the distance of the next thread from the first. Continue this process until the frame

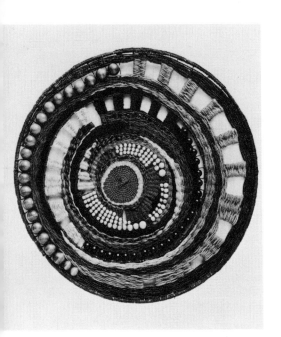

Fig. 19–6. Round weave. When weaving the first few circles the centre of the weave was pulled slightly to one side to create an interesting irregular effect. The radial warps, filled with beads, are very visible. In the centre a couple of rows of beads were woven one on top of the other to vary the structure.

forming an integral part of it. A disk-shaped wooden frame can also remain in the weave, but the nails must be knocked in on the underside.

On square frames the distances between the warp threads are easy to regulate. Obviously the threads must run parallel to each other, but the distances between them can be altered by doing more or less looping or by placing the nails further apart. This can produce exciting effects in the finished pattern because larger beads or additional smaller beads can be used in the spaces where the threads lie furthest apart, or the spaces can simply be left open in the work. You can decide which you prefer either in a sketch before starting work or during the actual weaving.

The weaving itself is very simple: string a long thread of a particular colour on a weaving needle. Then pass the weft to and fro, up and down, through one warp thread at a time. (The pattern can be varied by passing through every other warp thread.) The colours must harmonize, however, or the total effect will be untidy. If the frame is to remain in the finished weave you can leave large open spaces.

If you want to remove the frame the weave should be much more compact, or the texture will be too loose, and the weave will not hang nicely. In fact, rather than removing the weave from the frame, it is often preferable to use an ordinary weaving board. This consists simply of a board with a lath attached to each end, in both of which a number of nails with small heads are fixed at intervals. When you have completed the work, it is easy to remove from the board for finishing-off.

Whether working on a circular or a square frame, you should always be prepared to experiment (fig. 19–7). There are no rules for how the weaving can or should be done. Every method presents its own problems and its own solutions. You should assess the possibilities offered by different materials and start from there.

is full. You cannot set up the warp by winding it directly round the frame; it would become much too loose, and the threads would tend to pull towards the middle. This is why it is preferable to use looping, which secures the warp tightly to the frame (fig. 19–4). Another way of making a square frame is to hammer a few laths together (fig. 19–5).

The sides on which the warp is secured should be made of thicker wood than the others, since they must hold the nails to which the warp threads are fastened. Knot the thread to the first nail, then pass it round the wood to the nail on the opposite side, round this nail and back again, until the frame is full. This frame also remains in the finished weave,

20. More advanced bead-work

There are many possibilities for extending the techniques described in this book.

Making your own beads

You can substitute different materials for ready-made beads, such as shells, sgraffiato or sgraffito clay beads, or painted beans and pips. The following beans and pips can be made into beads: white and red beans; marrowfat, grey, and green peas; broad beans; and vetch, maize, sunflower, melon, apple, and orange pips. Pigeon feed and other rough poultry feeds can also be used. Use old beans and pips; new ones may start to sprout if they become damp.

To dye these beads, use a reputable brand of textile dye. Dissolve the dye in hot water in a rustproof container, and dilute it with enough cold water to cover all the beans. Leave the beans and pips in the dye until they become soft and swollen. (This process can take 12–24 hours, sometimes even longer.) Then remove them from the dye, and dry them thoroughly on newspaper covered with absorbent lavatory or kitchen paper. (This precaution will prevent the print on the newspaper from coming off on the surface of the beans.)

Now string the beans or pips on to a thin woollen thread with a large-eyed darning needle. Double and knot the thread to keep the beans from falling off. Push as many beans as possible down towards the end of the thread, making sure that the needle does not pass between the seed-lobes, since this would split the beans apart. Fill the thread up to within 1 in. (2·5 cm.) from the end, and put it in the refrigerator for a few hours (not in the freezing compartment – the beans would burst open)! Then put the thread in a cool, airy place to dry quickly. After a couple of hours, move the beans about on the thread to keep them from sticking. After several days (depending upon the climate), the beans will be almost ready;

spray them first with tanning oil, allowing it to soak in long enough to give them a permanent deep gloss, and then with hair-lacquer to make them water-proof. By following this procedure you can build a reserve of home-made beads which you can then use in all sorts of ways (fig. 20–1). Store any beans which you are not going to use immediately on their threads.

Page 91.
Fig. 19–7. Small wall decoration. This was woven freely without a pattern.

Opposite.
Fig. 20–1. Neck ornament. This was woven on a Formica loom by the winding method. There were quite a large number of warp threads through which the weft in various shades of red, together with beads made from beans and pips, was woven. The warp was divided into two loops and a metal hook added to one of them to make the clasp.

Page 94.
Fig. 20–2. A metal frame to which some rough fabric was sewn; patterns were cut out or marked by tacking stitches or loose threads.

Page 95.
Fig. 20–3. Wall decoration with shells. A piece of loosely-woven fabric was stretched over a rectangular frame; the area of the fabric is about two-and-a-half times as large as the frame. The patterns were marked by stitches, then the horizontal threads were cut to the edge of the tacking. These threads were then removed and turned back on both sides. (They could also be unravelled and left hanging loosely at the front of the weave.) Threads from the rest of the fabric were used again for the newly-woven sections. Shells were woven into the work, and relief effects were created by weaving on some of the loose threads and leaving loops on the side. These loosely-woven decorations were then rolled up and the warp threads pushed through to the back of the material.

Weaving within a frame

This is another way to vary your bead-work. Stretch a piece of rough weave over a metal frame. The actual area of the weave should be much greater than the part enclosed by the frame. Sew the frame to a corner of the material, allowing the rest to hang loose. Since you are using a rough weave (for instance, a rough linen weave) you can pull threads out and use them later on the frame.

First tack a few simple patterns on the part of the material within the frame, (rectangular, oval, and round shapes are the easiest to work with, especially if you have little experience). Then cut out the pattern (fig. 20–2), and pull the threads out as far as the tacking stitches. These threads can either remain loose, giving the weave a fluffy look, or be pulled to the back of the material, giving a well-ordered, finished look to the surface.

All sorts of possibilities are offered by the open parts of the weave where only the wool is left. You can weave threads pulled from other sections of the fabric or additional matching threads through the warp. Or you can introduce different materials altogether, such as dyed or natural pips and shells (fig. 20–3). These are very decorative, and they give your work an individual character.

There are many ways of weaving these beads into the work; the choice depends primarily on personal taste. You do not have to weave all over the material; you can leave open spaces because the material will remain supported by the frame. You might add a few loose beads at the front of the weave, or thread some beads together to make a woven bead border. This band can even be made into a roll by pulling the warp back at the position where the thread holding the beads was originally attached. Hanging rolls of beads will relieve the woven work very nicely (fig. 20–3).

93

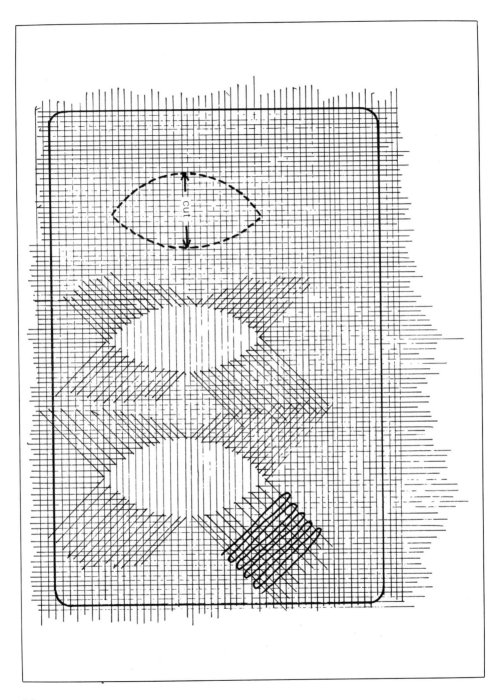

cut

Other Reinhold Craft Paperbacks

DOLLS AND TOY ANIMALS
Lis Albrectsen and Vibeke Lind

FLOWER DESIGNS IN CROSS-STITCH
Gerda Bengtsson and Elsie Thordur-Hansen

CROSS-STITCH PATTERNS IN COLOR
Gerda Bengtsson

PRINTMAKING WITHOUT A PRESS
Janet Erickson and Adelaide Sproul

METAL
John Hack

FREE WEAVING
Hoppe, Östlund and Melen

LEFT-HANDED NEEDLEPOINT
Regina Hurlburt

SIMPLE WEAVING
Grete Kroncke

POTTERY: RAKU TECHNIQUE
Finn Lynggaard

NEW DESIGNS IN LACE MAKING
Kristina Malmberg and Naime Thorlin

BATIK
Sara Nea

TIE DYE
Sara Nea

WOODCARVING
Walter Sack

COPPER, SILVER AND ENAMEL
Jan and Ove Sjöberg

IDEAS IN TEXTILES AND THREADS
Kerstin Sjodin

PATCHCRAFT
Elsie Svennas

WEAVING BANDS
Liv Trotzig and Astrid Axelsson

THE PILE WEAVES
Jean Wilson